Warning: This book is not

ISRAEL AND THE END OF THE WORLD

STEVE WOHLBERG

Remnant Publications

Warning: this book is not pro-Israel (at least not the nation of Israel, currently existing)

ISRAEL
AND THE
END OF THE WORLD

STEVE WOHLBERG

Israel and the End of the World has been made available to you by Remnant Publications (remnantpublications.com), Project Steps to Christ (www.projectstc.org), Amazing Facts (www.amazingfacts.org) and White Horse Media (www.whitehorsemedia.com)

Revised 2023

Published by
Remnant Publications, Inc.
649 East Chicago Road
Coldwater MI 49036
www.remnantpublications.com

Cover design by David Berthiaume
Text design by Greg Solie • Altamont Graphics

ISBN: 978-1-629133-10-2
SW1044

— Contents —

— Foreword —

The Bible is a book for all people, but it revolves around a specific people: the Jews. It is impossible to have a clear picture of final events without first having a correct understanding of the true place of the Jewish nation in prophecy.

As a Jewish Christian, I am deeply concerned about the widely accepted distortions regarding modern Israel and prophecy. When Jesus came the first time, the Jewish people were not prepared to receive Him because they had misunderstood the prophecies regarding His kingdom. When He died on the cross, even His own disciples were bewildered. They were looking for a literal kingdom in which the Messiah would overthrow their enemies so they could regain the earthly glory of Solomon's time. But when Jesus came the first time, He came to establish a spiritual kingdom (Luke 17:21).

Now, just before His second coming, the Christian world is repeating the Jewish nation's mistake. People are reversing the spiritual things to literal and then spiritualizing the plain letter! The tragedy is that in the process, they are setting themselves up for a devastating disappointment. Steve Wohlberg courageously exposes these popular yet dangerous misconceptions in a clear and progressive style that is irrefutable for honest Bible students. Pray, read, and then hold onto your seat!

—Doug Batchelor
Director of Amazing Facts
Radio and Television Ministries

— Author's Introduction —

This book is explosive. It's about Israel and Bible prophecy.

On October 7, 2023, black-scarfed militants belonging to a fierce group of Muslim terrorists calling themselves "Hamas" unexpectedly sprang out of the Gaza Strip into southern Israel to brutally murder nearly 1400 Israeli soldiers and civilians—including infants, children, youth, and the elderly. They also took over 200 hostages.

When the dust settled, the world stood aghast.

"Our country is at war with Hamas," quickly proclaimed Israeli Prime Minister Benjamin Netanyahu during a hastily called press conference. The Prime Minister also appealed to the United States for help. That same day, U.S. President Biden delivered a historic speech. "October 7 became the deadliest day for the Jewish people since the Holocaust," Biden declared, "and we will not stand by and do nothing again."[1] After condemning Hamas's evil savagery, Biden promised unreserved U.S. support for the ravaged State of Israel during that dark hour.

How did Christians respond? Appropriately, they reacted with shock, horror, and by sending up earnest prayers for the innocent and suffering. Yet many Christian leaders went further. In a short time, large numbers of pastors, authors, and well-known speakers quickly spoke on television, radio, and throughout social media declaring that these bloody events had more than of-this-world significance. Beyond bombs and human tragedy, they had pushed humanity one step closer to the Apocalyptic End of Days.

On Sunday morning, October 8, Pastor Greg Laurie at Harvest Christian Fellowship in Riverside, California, said this to a large audience:

> The Bible predicted thousands of years ago, that the end time events would revolve around Jerusalem. Not Irvine, not Riverside, not San Francisco, not Los Angeles, not Moscow, not Paris, but

1 See https://www.youtube.com/live/sYhnDPNwUhQ?si=y8N7N1ZEKF9oiY4y

> Jerusalem. This tiny little city in this tiny sliver of land will play a key role in the events of the last days … [2]

Two weeks later *The Roys Report* quoted bestselling Christian author Joel Richardson, who also confirmed his firm belief in the centrality of the Jewish state in biblical prophecy:

> One of the most essential realities, I think, for Christians when studying the Bible is to first understand the Israel-centric context," said Richardson. "All of the stories in the Bible primarily revolve around Jerusalem, Israel, and the larger Middle East. In the future, many of the great conflicts and controversies of the last days continue to revolve around Jerusalem. [3]

Near the close of the same month, Bloomberg also ran this headline: "Many Evangelicals See Israel-Hamas War as Part of a Prophecy." [4]

Such reports could be multiplied.

Whatever is happening in the Middle East by the time you read this, it is certainly true that the Israel/Jerusalem/prophecy connection is being regularly discussed worldwide on the Internet, in books, magazines, videos, on YouTube, on radio, on television, from the pulpit, in seminaries, and at prophecy conferences. And as global uncertainty and conflicts continue, we expect no letting up of this global trend.

While it is certainly true that there are differences of opinion today among Christian scholars who teach about earth's final days, it's no secret that large numbers are firmly convinced that the following five events have been plainly predicted in the pages of God's Word:

1. The rebirth of the State of Israel on May 14, 1948
2. The future rebuilding of a third Jewish temple on the Temple Mount in Jerusalem
3. A soon-coming "Seven-Year Period of Great Tribulation"

---

2 See https://youtu.be/5495g3NT4VA?si=fnAKUGuGds4EkVUN

3 *The Roys Report,* Oct. 19, 2023, "Christian Teachers Debate: Are Current Events in Israel Related to Biblical Prophecy?"

4 https://www.bloomberg.com/opinion/articles/2023-10-25/many-evangelicals-see-israel-hamas-war-as-part-of-a-prophecy?embedded-checkout=true

4. The rise of the Antichrist during this Tribulation, who will enter the rebuilt Jewish temple and proclaim that he is God

5. A final war against the nation of Israel, which will result in a Middle East-centered battle of Armageddon

Before going further, I wish to say that I also am Jewish, and that I love Jewish people. My mother, my father (both deceased), my brother, and my sister are all Jewish. During my upbringing in California, my family gathered to celebrate many Passover seders. At the end of my teenage years—it's a long story—I came to believe in Jesus Christ as my Messiah, Savior, and Lord. Today, as all Christians should, I also long to see both Jews and Arabs alike discover "The Prince of Peace" (Isaiah 9:6) who died for all of our sins and rose from the dead.

For the record, the purpose of this book isn't to attempt to solve a seemingly unsolvable Middle East mess, for I certainly don't have such wisdom. Instead, its assignment is to take a closer look at what the New Testament *really teaches* about Israel, Jerusalem, Jews, and Armageddon.

Just to be clear, the book of Revelation *does* predict that the final battle of Armageddon will someday be fought, as it is written:

> And they gathered them together to the place called in Hebrew, Armageddon. (Revelation 16:16)

Yet amid current discussions about prophecy, Israel, and the the End of the World, I am convinced that there is *a big deception* afloat more dangerous than the massive underwater block of ice that sunk the Titanic. For the good of humanity, this deception must be unmasked. If it isn't, it could lead millions, not to the bottom of the Atlantic Ocean, but into "the lake of fire" (see Revelation 21:8).

Please read this book carefully and prayerfully.

Its message could save your life.

— CHAPTER 1 —

All Eyes on Israel

What is right is not always popular
and what is popular is not always right
—Albert Einstein (1879–1955)

After much hype, when the world's clocks finally ticked over to 12:01 a.m. on the fearful year A.D. 2000, it quickly became obvious that Y2K doomsday prophecies had failed. Earnest predictions about massive computer chaos, power disruptions, bank failures, stock markets crashing, nuclear missiles launching, and the resulting global terror, all proved to be false prophecies.

Is it possible that certain end-time predictions about Israel will also fail?

On that same New Year's Eve in 1999, Israeli police assembled in record numbers inside Jerusalem. They were determined to keep the peace in the midst of growing concerns about terrorism and the possible explosive actions of religious fanatics. Thousands of pilgrims and worshippers were crowding toward the Temple Mount and the Wailing Wall as news reporters from across the globe swarmed throughout the City of David. With the approach of the long expected new millennium, apocalyptic interest was at its height. Countless Christians were thinking, *If the arrival of the year 2000 has anything to do with Bible prophecy and the end of the world, then surely Jerusalem is the place to watch!*

Yet nothing happened.

Why are so many eyes fixed upon Jerusalem? There are many reasons, yet one big one is clear. The fact is, literally millions of Christians who study prophecy firmly believe Planet Earth's final events will one day swirl around the Middle East, Jerusalem, and the Jews. According to what is commonly understood, what happens to the modern nation of Israel is definitely connected with an upcoming bloody battle of Armageddon, the return of Jesus Christ, and the end of the age.

Simply google "Israel and Bible Prophecy." Myriads of websites will pop up. Type in the same words on YouTube to discover countless videos. Or visit Amazon.com. The list of books on this topic is endless. Truly, the buzz is global. According to Bible prophecy teachers everywhere, "Israel," "the last days," and "end-time prophecies" are inseparably related. Bestselling apocalyptic author Carl Gallups told *World Net Daily*:

> In the end of it all, it's all about the return of Jesus Christ… He came the first time, according to the prophecies, and those same prophecies declare He is coming again. *Not only that, the prophecies are clear that He would return in the days shortly after Israel returned to the land, Jerusalem was in control of that returned Israel, and the Ezekiel 38 nations began their alignment against Israel.* Those days are here, and we are the first historical generation to see it happen …[5]

I realize that it may sound like blasphemy to some, but the purpose of this book is to re-examine the accuracy of these popular teachings, especially in the blazing light of Jesus Christ, of the New Testament, and the book of Revelation. What does Bible prophecy *really teach?* In the following pages, you will discover shocking yet biblical answers.

In our journey we will tackle these core questions:

- What did the Master mean when He said of Nathaniel, "Behold, an *Israelite indeed*, in whom is no deceit!"? (John 1:47, italics added).

- What did Paul have in mind when he wrote, "They are not all Israel who are of Israel"? (Romans 9:6).

- Why does the New Testament refer to *two Israels:* an "Israel after the flesh" (1 Corinthians 10:18) and "the Israel of God" (Galatians 6:14–16) in Jesus Christ?

- Finally, what is the true meaning of Revelation's mysterious prophecies about 144,000 from all the tribes of Israel, Mystery

5 See http://www.wnd.com/2016/09/messianic-preparations-underway-as-3rd-temple-planned/, italics added.

> Babylon, the Euphrates River drying up, and Armageddon, "the battle of the great day of God Almighty"? (Revelation 16:14–16).

Before diving deeper, I want to say again that I am Jewish. I abhor anti-semitism and love Jewish people. But sadly, most Jews today do not believe the Good News of Jesus Christ. They don't realize that Jesus Himself lived a perfect Jewish life and that His death fulfilled ancient Jewish prophecies about the birth, sinless life, suffering, death, and resurrection of their own Jewish Messiah (see Micah 5:2 and Isaiah 53). Like Paul, "my heart's desire and prayer to God for Israel is that they may be saved" (Romans 10:1)..

But here's a key point. In the midst of my love for Jewish people and Israel, I am also a student of prophecy. And in my research, I have come to a frightening conclusion. I am convinced that in the midst of popular prophetic theories about the modern Israeli nation, the war-torn city of Jerusalem, and Armageddon, there are actually gigantic errors—*false prophecies*—now being taught worldwide which are not in harmony with the exact words of Jesus Christ or with the true meaning of the book of Revelation. To His Jewish disciples our Lord warned, "Take heed that no one deceives you" (Matthew 24:4). As a Jewish believer, I have taken this warning seriously.

Y2K prophecies failed. No terrorist explosions took place in Jerusalem on the eve of the new millennium.

You are about to discover solid New Testament proof that many popular predictions about modern Israel will also fail. Yet God's Word will be fulfilled.

As you keep reading this book, this label is appropriate, "Warning: Handle with Prayer!"

— CHAPTER 2 —
Wrestling with an Angel

Humility, that low, sweet root,
from which all heavenly virtues shoot.
—Thomas Moore (1779–1852)

Have you ever heard of a wrestling match between a human being and an angel? As far as we know, it happened only once in history. The details of this ancient story will soon take on explosive significance in our study of Israel and Bible prophecy.

Abraham lived about 4,000 years ago. He had a son named Isaac who had a son named Jacob. It was Jacob who wrestled with the angel. As a result of that wrestling match, the angel changed Jacob's name to "Israel." In order to understand this strange encounter and its deep meaning for us today, we must study some history about Isaac, Rebekah, Esau, and Jacob as recorded in Genesis 27.

"When Isaac was old, and his eyes were dim, so that he could not see," he decided to bless Esau, his firstborn son, before he died (Genesis 27:1–4). But first he sent Esau out to the field to hunt for a tasty meal. Isaac's wife, Rebekah, had other plans. Realizing the importance of her husband's blessing upon the firstborn, she coveted that blessing for her younger son, Jacob, who was more spiritually-focused than Esau. While Esau was out hunting in the field, Rebekah quickly prepared a meal and convinced Jacob to take the food to Isaac while pretending to be Esau (Genesis 27:5–17).

When Jacob took the meal to his father, he lied, saying, "I am Esau thy firstborn; I have done according as thou badest me: arise, I pray thee, sit and eat of my venison, that thy soul may bless me" (verse 19). When Isaac inquired how it was that he had killed an animal so quickly, Jacob lied again, saying, "Because the Lord thy God brought it to me" (verse 20). Suspiciously, Isaac asked, "Art thou my very son Esau?" Jacob lied a third time, saying, "I am" (verse 24). Isaac finally believed Jacob's deception and gave him the blessing (verses 25–29).

Soon afterward, Esau returned from the hunt and Isaac realized he'd been tricked. "Thy brother came with subtilty, and hath taken away thy blessing" (verse 35), the father said to his older son. Then "Esau hated Jacob" and said in his heart, "I will slay my brother Jacob" (verse 41). Rebekah discovered Esau's plot and sent Jacob away to her relatives in a far country, where he remained for 20 years (Genesis 27:43; 31:41). Jacob never saw his mother's face again.

Twenty years later, Jacob headed home. Surrounded by a large caravan of family and servants, he sent messengers ahead of the group to tell Esau he was coming. But the men returned with the news that Esau and 400 soldiers were on their way to meet *him*. Fear gripped Jacob's heart. He felt a deep sense of guilt over his past sin of deception and was terrified for the safety of his family. So Jacob "rose up that night" and "was left alone" to plead with God for forgiveness and deliverance (Genesis 32:22, 24).

Then "there wrestled a man with him until the breaking of the day" (vs. 24). This man was really "the Angel" (Hosea 12:4). Unaware of this, and assuming this must be his still-angry brother Esau, Jacob struggled for his life all night. At the crack of dawn, this powerful Stranger revealed himself not as a foe, but as a heavenly Friend. He touched Jacob's thigh, "and the hollow of Jacob's thigh was out of joint, as he wrestled with him" (Genesis 32:25).

Jacob suddenly realized that this powerful Being was now his only hope. Broken and helpless, he clung to the Messenger, saying, "I will not let thee go, except thou bless me."

The angel then asked, "What is your name?"

"And he said, 'Jacob.'

"And he said, 'Thy name shall be called no more Jacob, *but Israel*: for as a prince hast thou power with God and with men, and hast prevailed'" (verses 26–28, italics added).

This is the *first time* the word "Israel" is used in the Bible. The context reveals its deep spiritual significance. In the beginning, "Israel" was a special name given to only one man, to Jacob, by an Angel of God. In the Bible, people's names mean more than they do today. Back then, names were often descriptions of people's characters.

Jacob literally meant "deceiver" or "crook." When Esau discovered Jacob's sin of deception, he said to Isaac, "Is he not rightly named Jacob" Genesis 27:36)? Thus the name, "Jacob," was a description of his character and of his sin. When the Angel asked, "What is your name," he knew the answer. But He wanted Jacob to say his own name, which represented a humble confession and turning away from his sin. Jacob passed the test, repented, and placed his entire dependence upon God's love and mercy.

The response, "Thy name shall no more be called Jacob, but Israel," revealed that God had given him a new character. The word "Israel" literally means "Prince with God" (see the margin of the New King James Version). Thus the name "Israel" itself was a spiritual name, symbolizing Jacob's spiritual victory over his past sin of deception. In other words, the man "Jacob" was now a spiritual "Israel." As we shall see, this truth about a spiritual Israel will take on explosive significance in our study of Israel and Bible prophecy.

Israel had 12 sons "which came into Egypt" (Exodus 1:1–5). One son, named Joseph, had vivid dreams (Genesis 37). Remember this, for we will come back to it. The children of Israel multiplied in Egypt and were forced into slavery until the time of Moses. Then God told Moses, "Say unto Pharaoh, Thus says the Lord, Israel is my son, even my firstborn.… Let my son go." (Exodus 4:22–23).

Here's an important development in biblical thought. The name "Israel" is now being expanded. It no longer refers only to Jacob, but also to his descendants. The nation is now "Israel." Thus, "Israel" first applied to a victorious man, then to a people. It was God's desire that this new nation of Israel should also be victorious, as was Jacob, through faith in Him. God called this new nation, "my son … my firstborn." Remember this also. It will become important shortly.

The next paragraph contains small phrases about Israel which may seem dry at first. But amazing things can happen when you water a dry seed. Those little phrases will soon sprout and grow into trees of towering significance when we turn to the New Testament. Take special note of them.

> Israel was "a vine" God brought "out of Egypt" (Psalm 80:8).
>
> God said, "But you, Israel, are my servant … the seed of Abraham" (Isaiah 41:8, NKJV).
>
> God also spoke of "Israel My elect" (Isaiah 45:4).

Again, the Lord spoke through Isaiah, saying, "Behold my servant, whom I uphold; mine elect, in whom my soul delights; I have put my spirit upon him: he shall bring forth judgment to the Gentiles. He shall not cry, nor lift up, nor cause his voice to be heard in the street. A bruised reed shall he not break, and the smoking flax shall he not quench: he shall bring forth judgment unto truth" (Isaiah 42:1–3).

All of these words originally applied to the literal nation of Israel. Don't forget this.

In about 800 B.C. the Lord said through the prophet Hosea, "When Israel was a child, then I loved him, and called my son out of Egypt" (Hosea 11:1). Yet by this time, Israel had failed to live up to the meaning of its own name. It had not lived victoriously, as a "Prince with God." The Lord sadly declared, "…They sacrificed unto Baalim, and burned incense to graven images" (Hosea 11:2).

Yet God had a special plan. That solitary sentence, "When Israel was a child, then I loved him, and called my son out of Egypt," is actually like a mini-bomb that will soon explode with tremendous importance as we turn to the New Testament.

— CHAPTER 3 —

A New Look at Jesus Christ

The voyage of discovery is not in seeking new landscapes but in having new eyes.
—Marcel Proust (1871–1922)

Approximately 800 years had passed since the time of Hosea the prophet. Finally, Heaven's prophetic clock struck twelve: "Jesus was born in Bethlehem of Judea in the days of Herod the king. …" (Matthew 2:1).

Because King Herod felt threatened by this newly born potential rival to his throne, he sent soldiers who cruelly "slew all the children that were in Bethlehem" (Matthew 2:16). Yet God warned Joseph in advance of the slaughter. "Behold, the angel of the Lord appeareth to Joseph in a dream, saying, Arise, and take the young child and his mother, and flee into Egypt, and be thou there until I bring thee word" (verse 13). So the family arose and "departed into Egypt" (verse 14).

The next sentence after Matthew 2:14 is almost unbelievable in its prophetic implications. Under the inspiration of the Holy Spirit, Matthew wrote that Joseph, Mary, and Jesus remained in Egypt "until the death of Herod: that it might be fulfilled which was spoken of the Lord by the prophet, saying, Out of Egypt have I called my son" (verse 15).

Do you realize what you just read? Matthew is quoting Hosea 11:1, which, in its historical context, referred to the nation of Israel being called out of Egypt in the time of Moses. Yet here the very first writer of the New Testament picks up this text and declares it "fulfilled" in Jesus Christ! Here Matthew is beginning to reveal a principle developed throughout his book. Paul also taught the same principle, as we shall see.

Remember, the first time the name "Israel" is used in the Bible it was a spiritual name given to one man: Jacob (Genesis 32:28). That name had to do with Jacob's spiritual victory. It meant, "Prince with God." Even so, in the beginning of the New Testament that same name is beginning to be applied to one Man, to the Victorious One, to Jesus Christ, *the* Prince of God.

There are amazing parallels between the history of Israel and the history of Jesus:

In Hebrew history a young man named Joseph had dreams and went to Egypt (Genesis 37, 39).

In the New Testament we find another Joseph who had dreams and went to Egypt (Matthew 2).

In Hebrew history, when God called Israel out of Egypt, He called that new nation "my son" (Exodus 4:22).

When Jesus came out of Egypt, God said, "Out of Egypt I have called my son" (Matthew 2:15).

When the nation of Israel left Egypt, the people went through the Red Sea. They were "baptized… in the sea" (1 Corinthians 10:2).

In the third chapter of Matthew, we read that Jesus was baptized in the Jordan "to fulfill all righteousness" (verse 15). Then God called Jesus, His "beloved Son" (verse 17).

After the Israelites passed through the Red Sea, they spent 40 years in the wilderness. Immediately after Jesus was baptized in the Jordan, He was "led up of the Spirit into the wilderness" for 40 days (Matthew 4:1–2). At the end of those 40 days, Jesus resisted the devil's tricky temptations by quoting three Scriptures. All were from Deuteronomy, the very book God gave Israel during her 40-year sojourn in the wilderness! What does this mean? It means that in Matthew's book, Jesus was repeating the history of Israel, point by point, and was overcoming where they failed. In other words, Christ was showing Himself to be *the* primary Israel, *the* Prince of God, *the* Victorious One who overcomes all sin.

After healing large numbers of people, Jesus "charged them that they should not make him known: That it might be fulfilled which was spoken by Esaias the prophet, saying, Behold my servant, whom I have chosen; my beloved, in whom my soul is well pleased: I will put my spirit upon him, and he shall shew judgment to the Gentiles. He shall not strive, nor cry; neither shall any man hear his voice in the streets. A bruised reed shall he not break, and smoking flax shall he not quench, till he send forth judgment unto victory" (Matthew 12:16–20).

Here Matthew is doing the same thing he did with Hosea 11:1. He is quoting Isaiah 42:1–3 which, in its original context, referred to God's "servant," which was "Israel… my servant" (Isaiah 41:8). Once again, under inspiration from the Holy Spirit, the first writer of the New Testament said that Isaiah 42:1–3 had been "fulfilled" by God's "servant," Jesus Christ.

What about those other seemingly dry little phrases about the nation of Israel? It's time to water them, too. They must now grow into trees that reach heaven.

In Psalm 80:8, Israel was called a "vine." Yet Jesus Christ declared, "I am the true vine" (John 15:1).

God referred to the nation of Israel as "My son, even My firstborn" (Exodus 4:22). Yet Paul later called Jesus Christ "the firstborn of every creature" (Colossians 1:15).

The prophet Isaiah clearly called Israel "the seed of Abraham" (Isaiah 41:8). Yet Paul wrote, "Now to Abraham and his seed were the promises made. He saith not, And to seeds, as of many; but as of one, And to thy seed, which is Christ" (Galatians 3:16).

That last text is the clearest and most explosive of them all. What does this mean? It means that when Paul looked back at Old Testament statements about "Israel," he saw them as inherently foreshadowing the coming Messiah, Jesus Christ. To Paul, the Messiah is "the Seed."

Jesus Christ is the perfect Israel!

Yet there's more. In Genesis and Exodus the name "Israel" not only referred to one victorious man, to Jacob, but also to his descendants, who became Israel. The same principle is revealed in the New Testament. Right after calling Jesus "the Seed," Paul told his Gentile converts, "And if you be Christ's, then are you Abraham's seed…." (Galatians 3:29). Thus in the New Testament, the name Israel not only applies to the one Victorious Man, the true Seed, Jesus Christ, but also to those who are in Christ. Believers in Jesus are infused into the "Seed." In other words, true Christians are part of God's spiritual Israel.

God made a covenant with the twelve tribes of Israel at the foot of Mount Sinai. Animal sacrifices were offered. Then "Moses took the blood, and sprinkled it on the people, and said, Behold the blood of the covenant, which the Lord hath made with you…" (Exodus 24:8). At the end of His ministry, Jesus Christ made a new covenant with the twelve apostles in an upper room on Mount Zion. Before offering Himself as the Final Sacrifice, our Lord declared, "This is my blood of the new testament [covenant], which is shed for many for the remission of sins" (Matthew 26:28).

What does this mean? It means that Jesus Christ, the true Seed, was making a new covenant with His spiritual Israel.

These fundamental New Testament facts will soon take on explosive significance when we examine what the book of Revelation *really teaches* about Israel, Babylon the Great, and Armageddon.

May I suggest you put your seatbelts on?

— CHAPTER 4 —

Clarity Through Double Vision

Beware of the half-truth. You may have gotten hold of the wrong half.
—Author Unknown

Have you ever been hit so hard on the head you started seeing double? From what I have studied, the Christian world needs to get hit hard on the head with the truth of the New Testament. Then more Christians will start seeing double about the subject of Israel. According to Paul, there are two Israels. The proof? The Jewish apostle wrote, "They are not all Israel, which are of Israel" (Romans 9:6). In this chapter, we will discover that there is an "Israel after the flesh" (1 Corinthians 10:18) and an "Israel of God" (Galatians 6:16) composed of both Jews and Gentiles who have personal faith in Jesus Christ, God's true Messiah.

Paul wrote, "Even as Abraham believed God, and it was accounted to him for righteousness. Know ye therefore that they which are of faith, the same are the children of Abraham" (Galatians 3:6–7). Paul's argument is that Abraham had faith, therefore those who have faith are his children. We might call this the concept of "faith lineage." This truth is like a key that can open a lock in our heads. Once the lock is open, we can understand the shocking principle of two Israels.

John the Baptist understood and boldly preached faith lineage. When a group of tricky Pharisees and Sadducees came to question John's right to baptize, the wilderness prophet astonished them by shouting, "Think not to say within yourselves, We have Abraham to our father: for I say unto you, that God is able of these stones to raise up children unto Abraham. And now also the axe is laid unto the root of the trees: therefore every tree which bringeth not forth good fruit is hewn down, and cast into the fire" (Matthew 3:9–10).

Those Pharisees and Sadducees were Israelites "after the flesh" (1 Corinthians 10:18). They did not have faith like Abraham did, yet they claimed to be his children. John the Baptist exposed this illusion. "Don't think that!" he thundered. John then laid the "axe" to the root of the trees by saying that if they didn't bear "good fruit" through faith in God like Abraham did, they would be "hewn down, and cast into the fire" (verse 10).

Clearly natural lineage alone is not enough. Without faith and a spiritual connection with the Almighty, those men were doomed.

Jesus Christ taught the same truth. A certain group of Jewish people once said to Him, "Abraham is our father." Jesus responded, "If ye were Abraham's children, ye would do the works of Abraham" (John 8:39). They also claimed to be Abraham's children, but they had no faith. By saying, "*If* ye were Abraham's children," Jesus denied their claim. Christ continued, "But now ye seek to kill me, a man that hath told you the truth … this did not Abraham. Ye do the deeds of your father…" (John 8:40–41).

They responded, "We have one Father, even God." Then "Jesus said unto them, If God were your Father, ye would love me…Ye are of your father the devil, and the lusts of your father ye will do. He was a murderer from the beginning, and abode not in the truth, because there is no truth in him. When he speaketh a lie, he speaketh of his own: for he is a liar, and the father of it" (John 8:41–42, 44).

What an atomic text! Here Jesus Christ spoke words that blast into slivers a prophetic theory currently held in the evangelical world. Jesus was talking to some Jewish people who claimed to be Israelites, the children of Abraham, yet they were only following God outwardly, not in heart. Jesus said they weren't really Abraham's children at all because they had no faith and were following lies. Their "faith lineage" actually went back to Satan, the father of lies. Soon we will separate God's truth from Satan's lies when we look at what Revelation *really teaches* about Israel, the 144,000, Mystery Babylon, and Armageddon.

Jesus Christ also taught faith lineage in John 1. A spiritually-minded Jew named Nathanael was wondering whether Jesus of Nazareth was really his Messiah. Retiring to a favorite spot under a fig tree, he prayed about the matter. Soon a friend introduced him to the Savior. When Jesus saw Nathanael, He joyfully declared, "Behold an Israelite indeed, in whom is no guile!" (John 1:47).

Nathanael had a natural lineage that went back to Abraham. Yet he had more. In his spiritual life he had gained victories over "guile," which means deception. When Jesus discerned Nathanael's spiritual lineage to Abraham and Jacob, He called him "an Israelite indeed." Just as Jacob himself had become a spiritual Israel, even so had Nathanael become "an Israelite indeed." He was part of God's true spiritual Israel.

Just as there are two Israels, even so are there two kinds of Jews. There are Jewish people in the flesh and Jewish people in the Spirit. In words of warning to certain Jews who were breaking the Ten Commandments, Paul wrote, "Behold, thou art called a Jew, and restest in the law, and makest thy boast of God… For circumcision verily profiteth, if thou keep the law: but if thou be a breaker of the law, thy circumcision is made uncircumcision. Therefore if the uncircumcision [Gentiles] keep the righteousness of the law, shall not his uncircumcision be counted for circumcision?… For he is not a Jew, which is one outwardly; neither is that circumcision, which is outward in the flesh: But he is a Jew, which is one inwardly; and circumcision is that of the heart, in the spirit, and not in the letter; whose praise is not of men, but of God" (Romans 2:17, 25–26, 28–29).

Did you catch that? Someone who is "called a Jew" because he is a physical descendant of Abraham, and yet who lives as a lawbreaker, is "not a Jew." His "circumcision is made uncircumcision." To God, he is a Gentile. And the believing Gentile, who through faith keeps "the righteousness of the law," his uncircumcision is "counted for circumcision." To God, he's a Jew. Thus John the Baptist, Jesus Christ and Paul all agree — natural lineage is not enough.

Whether or not someone is "an Israelite indeed" depends upon one's faith and spiritual character. Paul summarized, "For we are the circumcision, which worship God in the spirit, and rejoice in Christ Jesus, and have no confidence in the flesh" (Philippians 3:3). Anyone today can become one of these "Jews," no matter who their earthly parents are.

These concepts of faith lineage, Jews being counted as Gentiles, and vice versa, lead us to one of the biggest issues facing the prophecy-minded Christian world. This issue is at the core of prophetic interpretation. In it, we are faced with two options. One is the truth, the other a lie. One leads to heaven and the other, possibly, to hell.

The question is, "What about the promises God made to Israel in the Old Testament?" If we conclude those promises must be fulfilled to Israel after the flesh, then we must conclude that Jerusalem and the modern Jewish nation will eventually become the epicenter of the final battle of Armageddon. But if we conclude that those promises can legitimately be fulfilled to God's Israel in the Spirit, then we must restudy the book of Revelation to discover how its end-time prophecies apply to true Christians—Jewish or Gentile—who love Jesus the Messiah with all their hearts.

Paul deals with this explosive issue in Romans 9:2–8. His words require careful thought. Sorrowfully, Paul wrote about his Jewish "kinsman according to the flesh: Who are Israelites; to whom pertaineth the adoption, and the glory, and the covenants, and the giving of the law, and the service of God, and the promises" (verses 2–4). God did make promises to Israel in the Old Testament. Yet what if some Jews do not believe in Him? Can God fulfill His promises to an unbelieving Israel after the flesh? If not, has His Word failed?

Paul's answer to these important questions is vital: "Not as though the word of God hath taken none effect. For they are not all Israel, which are of Israel" (verse 6). Notice that the truth of "two Israels" is Paul's assurance that God's Word will not fail. Look carefully: "They are not all Israel [the Israel of God], which are of Israel [of the Jewish nation]." Thus a Jew can be of the Jewish nation and yet not be part of the Israel of God. Now here's the explosive question: To *which Israel* will God fulfill His promises?

Paul continues: "Neither, because they are the seed of Abraham, are they all children: but, In Isaac shall thy seed be called" (verse 7). Since not all physical descendants of Abraham are automatically God's children, therefore His promises are for those "in Isaac."

Abraham had two sons. The first was Ishmael, who was born after the flesh. The second was Isaac, who was born when Abraham had faith in God's promise (Genesis 16:1–3, 15; 21:1–3; Romans 4:18–21). In Galatians 4:22–31, Paul shockingly reveals that Ishmael *represents* unbelieving Jews, while Isaac *represents* Jews and Gentiles who have faith in Christ! "Now we, brethren [as believers in Christ], as Isaac was, are the children of promise" (Galatians 4:28).

The "children of promise" are those who "receive the promise of the Spirit through faith" (Galatians 3:14). Therefore, the Israel that is "in Isaac" is the Israel of God in the Holy Spirit. Paul concludes, "That is, they which are the children of the flesh, these are not the children of God: but the children of the promise are *counted for the seed*" (Romans 9:8, italics added). "Counted for the seed" means that, although some may be Gentiles, they're in.

Here is an eight-point summary of Paul's detailed reasoning:

1. God made promises to "the seed" of Abraham (Galatians 3:16)
2. Abraham's seed would continue "in Isaac" (Romans 9:7)
3. Isaac was born when Abraham had faith in God's promise (Romans 4:19–21)
4. Isaac *represents* everyone who believes in Jesus and receives the promise of the Holy Spirit by faith (Galatians 3:14; 4:22–28)
5. *All* who have faith in Jesus Christ—Jews or Gentiles—"are counted as the seed" (Galatians 3:14; Romans 9:8; 10:12)
6. This seed is "the Israel of God" in Christ (Galatians 3:16, 29; 6:14–16)
7. God will fulfill His promises to *this Israel* (Galatians 3:29; 4:28; 6:14–16)
8. Thus God's promises to Israel have not been made of "none effect," even though some natural Jewish people don't believe in their own Messiah (Romans 9:6–8)

Here we have the answer to the issue that means so much in prophetic interpretation. The Bible is clear. God will fulfill His Old Testament promises to those "in Isaac"—that is, to *any human being* who follows Abraham's example and who becomes part of His Israel in the Spirit through faith in the Messiah. Thus the issue is not race, bloodline, genealogy, or ethnicity, but personal faith—a faith now available to all (Romans 10:12).

Those who are only "the children of flesh, these are not the children of God: but the children of the promise are counted for the seed" (Romans 9:8). We should not expect God to fulfill His promises to unbelieving Israelites of the flesh (or to lips-only Christians of the flesh, for that matter), unless, of course, they individually become true believers in the Messiah.

Let's look at one more controversial section before we close this chapter. What about Paul's question, "Hath God cast away his people? ..." (Romans 11:1). These words are being quoted around the world to prove that God has not cast away any Israelites of the flesh. First of all, the same chapter does describe "the casting away" of some who don't believe (verse 15). Second, reading further in verse 1, notice carefully Paul's answer to his own question: "God forbid. For I also am an Israelite, of the seed of Abraham..." Thus Paul uses himself as an example to prove that God has not "cast away his people."

Who are "His people"?

In the next three verses, Paul refers to Israel's apostasy in the days of Elijah. God said to Elijah, "I have reserved to myself seven thousand men, who have not bowed the knee to the image of Baal" (verse 4). In Elijah's time there were also two Israels. One followed Baal, the other followed God.

Then Paul made this application. "Even so then at this present time also there is a remnant according to the election of grace" (verse 5). Just as in Elijah's time there was a faithful remnant of Israel, even so in Paul's time there was also a faithful remnant of believing Jews, who, like himself, had been saved by grace. In the Old Testament, the Lord said to those who followed idols, "...you are not My people" (Hosea 1:9). But to those who experience the New Covenant and have His law in their hearts, He says, "They shall be My people" (Hebrews 8:10, NKJV). It is this faithful remnant of Israel, composed of Jewish people like Paul, which God has certainly not "cast away."

Soon we will see this exact issue addressed in the mysterious book of Revelation. As in the days of Elijah, we are now in the midst of a terrible apostasy. Yet today God has His "seven thousand" who haven't "bowed the knee to Baal." They are His faithful remnant, His Israel in the Holy Spirit, who rely on God's power instead of their flesh. Like Elijah, they will be on the side of Jesus Christ and His truth at Armageddon.

— CHAPTER 5 —

Choice and the Chosen Nation

Man has no choice but to choose...
—Jean Paul Sartre (1905–1980)

From the summit of Mount Sinai, God Almighty thundered to Moses: "'Thus shalt thou say to the house of Jacob, and tell the children of Israel; Ye have seen what I did unto the Egyptians, and how I bare you on eagles' wings, and brought you unto myself. Now therefore, if ye will obey my voice indeed, and keep my covenant, then ye shall be a peculiar treasure unto me above all people: for all the earth is mine: And ye shall be unto me a kingdom of priests, and an holy nation'" (Exodus 19:3–6).

Notice the words "if" and "then." God said that "if" Israel obeyed, "then" they would be His "peculiar treasure." That tiny word "if" involves a mega issue. It concerns conditions. God loved Israel and chose her apart from any obedience on her part. He brought the people out of Egypt, bore them on eagles' wings, and brought them to Himself. Yet, contrary to popular opinion, God's use of "if" made it clear that the continuation of His favor to the Israelites was conditional upon their response to His goodness—upon their choices to obey (see also 1 Samuel 2:30; Jeremiah 18:7–10). In other words, those of the chosen nation must themselves choose correctly, or the consequences would be catastrophic.

Forty years later, Israel entered the Promised Land and remained there for about 800 years. During this period, many responded to God's love and chose to obey His voice. But the majority strayed from the path of righteousness. Again and again, God manifested His mercy by sending prophets and pleading with Israel to return to His covenant. Yet apostasy continued and deepened. Finally, after hundreds of years of warning, disaster struck. In 722 B.C., the northern tribes were assaulted and carried away by the cruel Assyrians. In 586 B.C., Judah was taken to Babylon. Such was the result of wrong choices.

In 586 B.C., the armies of Babylon demolished Jerusalem and burned its temple with fire. The Jews were removed from their land and carried into captivity. Yet, in the mercy of God, this exile was not to be permanent. The prophet Jeremiah predicted that God "would accomplish seventy years in the desolations of Jerusalem" (Daniel 9:2). After 70 years the Jews would leave Babylon, return to their land, and rebuild their temple and their city. God was giving His chosen nation another chance to respond to His love and make right choices. In simple terms, the Lord was saying, "You blew it. Let's try again!"

This new opportunity is revealed in a momentous prophecy of "seventy weeks." Near the end of the Babylonian captivity the angel Gabriel notified the prophet Daniel that "Seventy weeks are determined upon thy people and upon thy holy city, to finish the transgression, and to make an end of sins, and to make reconciliation for iniquity, and to bring in everlasting righteousness, and to seal up the vision and the prophecy, and to anoint the most Holy" (Daniel 9:24).

This 70-week prophetic period, based on the day-for-a-year principle recorded in Numbers 14:34 and Ezekiel 4:6, calculates out to 490 literal years. The entire period was "determined" for Daniel's people, the Jews. During that period, the chosen nation would have another chance "to finish the transgression" and "make an end of sins." Near the end of that period, something big would happen. Israel's Messiah would come "to bring in everlasting righteousness." As we shall soon see, Israel's status as a special nation under Divine favor would be determined by her choice to receive, or to reject, that Messiah.

Gabriel told Daniel exactly when the "seventy weeks" would begin. "Know therefore and understand," declared God's angel, "that from the going forth of the commandment to restore and to build Jerusalem unto the Messiah the Prince shall be seven weeks, and threescore and two weeks" (Daniel 9:25).

Persia conquered Babylon in 538 B.C. Shortly thereafter, the Persian King Cyrus issued a decree for the Jewish people to return to their land and rebuild their temple (Ezra 1:1–3). Later, King Darius issued another decree that led to the completion of the temple (Ezra 6:1, 8). Still later, King Artaxerxes gave Nehemiah permission to rebuild the demolished wall around the city (Nehemiah 1:3;

2:1–9). Yet the predicted "commandment to restore and to build Jerusalem" actually occurred a bit earlier when the same King Artaxerxes issued a lengthy decree, giving Ezra official authority to "set magistrates and judges" over Jerusalem and that "judgement be executed" upon all who refused to follow the laws of God and the king (Ezra 7:21, 25–26). Of these four options to consider as a starting point for the 70-week/490-year prophecy, King Artaxerxes' decree or commandment recorded in Ezra chapter 7 was the only one that fully restored civil authority to Jerusalem and the Jewish state.

That commandment occurred "in the seventh year of Artaxerxes" (Ezra 7:7), which was 457 B.C. This precise date (457 B.C.) is listed in the margin of Ezra 7 in many modern Bibles. The widely-acclaimed *Encyclopedia of Bible Difficulties* (Zondervan, 1982) also pinpoints 457 B.C. as the starting point of the 70-week prophecy.[6] The Angel Gabriel said, "From the going forth of the commandment to restore and to build Jerusalem unto the Messiah the Prince shall be seven weeks [49 years], and threescore [60] and two weeks [62 weeks = 434 years]" (Daniel 9:25).

7 weeks (49 years) + 62 weeks (434 years) = 69 weeks (483 years)

Going forward 483 years from the starting point of 457 B.C. comes to A.D. 27, the time of the appearance of "the Messiah the Prince" (Daniel 9:25). The word *Messiah* means "Anointed One," and in A.D. 27—the exact year specified in Gabriel's prophecy[7]—Jesus was "anointed" by the Holy Spirit at His baptism (Matthew 3:16, 17; Acts 10:38), thus officially beginning His public ministry.

Shortly after His baptism, our Savior declared, "*The time is fulfilled,* and the kingdom of God is at hand. Repent, and believe in the gospel" (Mark 1:15, NKJV, italics added). The Master's words, "the time is fulfilled," can refer to *no other time prophecy except Daniel 9:25.*

Jesus knew He was fulfilling that ancient prediction.

As we have seen, Gabriel's prophecy specified a total period of "seventy weeks" (Daniel 9:24). He then sub-divided that period into three smaller periods made up of seven weeks (verse 25), sixty-two weeks (verse 25), and then one final week (verse 27).

---

6 Gleason L. Archer, *Encyclopedia of Bible Difficulties* (Grand Rapids, MI: Zondervan, 1982), p. 290.

7 *Ibid*

7+62+1=70.

So far we have seen 69 weeks fulfilled, which leaves only "one week" left. That last week is often called "the 70th week of Daniel." That highly controversial text about that last week literally says:

> And he shall confirm the covenant with many for one week, and in the midst of the week he shall cause the sacrifice and the oblation to cease… (Daniel 9:27).

Based on the day-year principle, the "one week" remaining in this prophecy also refers to *a period of seven years*. Prophecy teachers often apply this to a future seven-year period of tribulation. Their idea is that while the first 69 weeks (or 483 years) did reach to the first coming of Jesus Christ, the prophetic clock then stopped because the Jewish people largely rejected Him. Then they catapult the 70th week (the last seven years) all the way down to the end-times, call it "the Tribulation," and say it will kick-in for the Jewish people after an event called "The Rapture" that will supposedly snatch all true Christians from this earth, taking them to heaven. Such teachers usually interpret Daniel 9:27 as follows:

> *"He shall confirm the covenant with many for one week."*
>
> "He" is applied to a future Antichrist who will make a covenant (or peace treaty) with the Jews during the seven years of Tribulation.
>
> *"In the midst of the week he shall cause the sacrifice and the oblation to cease…"*
>
> In the middle of the seven-year Tribulation, the Antichrist will break his covenant, turn against Israel, and stop their animal sacrifices.
>
> The phrase, *"he shall cause the sacrifice… to cease"* is viewed as irrefutable proof that a Jewish Temple *must* be rebuilt on the Temple Mount inside Jerusalem, that animal sacrifices *must* be restarted, and that a future Antichrist *will* stop those sacrifices during the Tribulation in fulfillment of Bible prophecy.

Therefore, according to countless modern interpreters, Daniel 9:27 is applied to a future Antichrist, a future peace treaty with Israel, a future seven-year Tribulation, and a future Jewish Temple inside Jerusalem. All of these events will supposedly start with the Rapture.

But think soberly for a moment. Really, that's an awful lot to extrapolate from a single Bible verse, *especially when Daniel 9:27 itself doesn't specifically say anything about a seven-year "Tribulation," "Antichrist," or a "rebuilt" Jewish temple.*

Could there be something wrong with this picture?

You'll find out in the next chapter.

After that, we'll look at the true significance of Jesus Christ's predicted appearance at the end of the 69 weeks/483 years to Israel's official status as God's chosen nation.

Again, seatbelts are highly recommended.

— CHAPTER 6 —

The 70th Week of Daniel Delusion

A lie can travel halfway around the world while the truth is still putting on its shoes.
—Mark Twain (1835–1910)

As you may be aware, prophecy-minded Christians all over Planet Earth sometimes engage in a fierce debate about whether Jesus Christ will return for His Church before the seven years of Tribulation (the "Pre-Trib" view), in the middle of the seven years (the "Mid-Trib" view), or at the end of the seven years (the "Post-Trib" view). Yet by far the most explosive question all too few seem to be asking is: "Is an end-time 'seven-year period of Tribulation' really the correct interpretation of Daniel 9:27 in the first place?"

In 1945, after months of agonizing deliberation, US President Harry Truman finally issued orders to drop two atomic bombs upon Japan during World War II. On August 6, the first bomb called the "Little Boy" fell on Hiroshima. Three days later another bomb called "Fat Man" was released over Nagasaki. Approximately 130,000 people were instantly vaporized. Many heated discussions have occurred as to whether or not it was the right thing to drop those bombs. One thing's for sure—in the minds of those who made that fearful decision, they believed it was for the ultimate good of America.

Dear friend, it is for the benefit of Christians everywhere that God's bomb of truth should now be released over what I have come to call "The 70th week of Daniel Delusion." Follow me closely. Daniel 9:27 literally says:

> He shall confirm the covenant with many for one week: and in the midst of the week he shall cause the sacrifice and the oblation to cease (Daniel 9:27).

This may shock you, but historically, the vast majority of well-respected Bible scholars and Bible commentaries have not applied Daniel 9:27 to a future seven-year period of "Tribulation" at all. Neither have they interpreted the "he" as referring to a future Mr. Deadly.

Instead, they applied it to *Jesus Christ.*

Notice what the world-famous Bible commentary by Matthew Henry says about Daniel 9:27:

> By offering himself a sacrifice once and for all he [Jesus] shall put an end to all the Levitical sacrifices."[8]

Matthew Henry applied Daniel 9:27 to *Christ*, not the Antichrist.

Another famous commentary by British Methodist Adam Clarke says that during Daniel 9:27's "term of seven years," Jesus Himself would "confirm or ratify the new covenant with mankind."[9]

Another well-known dusty Bible commentary reveals: "He shall confirm the covenant—Christ. The confirmation of the covenant is assigned to Him."[10]

Here's one more statement from an old book, *Christ and Antichrist*, published in 1846 by the Presbyterian Board of Publication. On page 2, under Recommendations, you'll find endorsements from Presbyterian, Methodist, and Baptist ministers, including an official representative of the Southern Baptist Convention.[11] Commenting on the final week of Daniel 9:27, that ancient volume states:

> …sometime during the remaining seven, he [the Messiah] was to die as a sacrifice for sin, and thus bring in "everlasting righteousness." Here are allusions to events so palpable, that one would think, the people among whom they occurred, could not possibly have misapplied the prophecy.[12]

---

8 Matthew Henry, *Commentary on the Whole Bible,* Vol. IV—*Isaiah to Malachi, Complete Edition* (New York: Fleming H. Revell Co., 1712), p. 1094, notes on Daniel 9:27

9 Adam Clarke, *The Holy Bible with a Commentary and Critical Notes*, Vol. IV, *Isaiah to Malachi* (New York: Abingdon-Cokesbury Press, ~1825), p. 602, notes on Daniel 9:27

10 Rev. Robert Jamieson, Rev. A.R. Fausset, and Rev. David Brown, *A Commentary Critical and Explanatory on the Whole Bible, Complete Edition* (Hartford, CN: S.S. Scranton Co., 1871), p. 641, notes on Daniel 9:27.

11 Samuel J. Cassels, *Christ and Antichrist* (Philadelphia, PA: Presbyterian Board of Publication, 1846), p. 2. (Reprinted by Hartland Publications, Rapidan, VA.)

12 *Ibid.*, p. 47.

Okay, here we go. The following 10 points provide logical and convincing evidence that Daniel's famous 70th week has no application to any future seven-year "Tribulation." Rather, this great prophetic period was perfectly fulfilled *2,000 years ago.*

1. The entire prophecy of Daniel 9:24–27 covers a period of "seventy weeks." Logic requires that "seventy weeks" refers to one consecutive block of time, in other words, to seventy *straight, sequential weeks.* The truth is, there is no example in Scripture (or anywhere else) of a stated time period starting, stopping, and then starting again. *All* biblical references to time are consecutive: 40 days and 40 nights (Genesis 7:4), 400 years in Egypt (Genesis 15:13), 70 years of captivity (Daniel 9:2), etc. In Daniel's prophecy, the "seventy weeks" were to begin during the reign of Persia and continue to the time of the Messiah.

2. Logic also requires that the 70th week follow immediately after the 69th week. If it doesn't, it cannot properly be called the 70th week!

3. It is illogical to insert a 2,000-year gap between the 69th and 70th week. No hint of a gap is found in the prophecy itself. There is no gap between the first seven weeks and the following 62 weeks, so why insert one between the 69th and 70th week?

Note: If you told your child to be in bed in 70 minutes, you obviously would mean 70 *consecutive* minutes. What if five hours later your son complained, "But dad, I know 69 minutes have passed, but the 70th minute hasn't started yet!"? (After receiving an appropriate reprimand, he would be swiftly sent to bed.)

4. Daniel 9:27 itself says nothing about a seven-year period of "Tribulation," a future rebuilt *Jewish* temple, or any "Antichrist" (the exact word, "*Antichrist,*" isn't even used until the New Testament).

5. The stated focus of the prophecy is *the Messiah*, not the Antichrist. After the Messiah is "cut off" (referring to Christ's death), the text says, "And the people of the prince

who is to come shall destroy the city and the sanctuary." In the past, this prediction has been consistently applied to the destruction of Jerusalem and the second temple by Roman armies led by Prince Titus in A.D. 70.[13]

6. "He shall confirm the covenant. ..." Paul said "the covenant" was "confirmed before by God in Christ" (Galatians 3:17). Jesus Christ came "to *confirm* the promises made to the fathers" (Romans 15:8, italics added). Daniel 9:27 doesn't say "*a* covenant" or peace treaty, but "*the* covenant" (KJV), which can only apply to the New Covenant. Nowhere in the Bible does the Antichrist make or confirm a covenant with anyone. The word "covenant" is Messianic, and *always* applies to the Messiah, not the Antichrist.

7. "He shall confirm the covenant with many." Jesus Christ said, "This is my blood of the new *covenant,* which is shed for *many*..." (Matthew 26:28, italics added). Behold, a perfect fit! Jesus was quoting Daniel 9:27 specifically.

8. "In the midst of the week he shall cause the sacrifice and the oblation to cease." After exactly three and a half years of holy ministry, Jesus Christ died on the cross "in the midst of the week [in the middle of the seven years]." At the exact moment of His death, "the veil of the temple was torn in two from the top to the bottom..." (Matthew 27:51).

This act of God signified that all animal sacrifices at that moment ceased to be of value. Why? Because the Perfect Sacrifice had been offered! Based on this wonderful event, God surely has no need for any future temple in Israel. Not only that, but if a temple ever was rebuilt, and if bloody animal sacrifices were resumed, that temple surely wouldn't be God's temple, for those very sacrifices would be an open denial of the perfect, once-for-all sacrifice of His Son. Thus, that temple *itself* would be *anti*-Christ.

9. "For the overspreading of abominations he shall make it desolate..." "The abomination of desolation" (see Matthew

13 See notes on Daniel 9:26 in commentaries by Matthew Henry (p. 1095), Adam Clarke (p. 603), and Jamieson, Fausset and Brown (p. 641).

24:15) is not a simple subject, yet we know that Jesus clearly applied this event to the time when His followers were to flee from Jerusalem before the destruction of the second temple in A.D. 70. In a parallel text to Matthew 24:15, Jesus told His disciples, "When you shall see Jerusalem compassed with armies [Roman armies led by Prince Titus], *then know that its desolation is near*" (Luke 21:20, NKJV, italics added). The disciples did "see" those very events. Because of the "abominations" of the Pharisees, Jesus told them, "Behold, your house is left unto you desolate" (Matthew 23:38). Thus, Gabriel's statement in Daniel 9:27 about Jerusalem becoming "desolate" was perfectly fulfilled in A.D. 70.

10. Gabriel said that the 70-week prophecy specifically applied to the Jewish people (Daniel 9:24). During the period of Christ's public ministry of three-and-a-half years, the Master's focus was largely upon "the lost sheep of the house of Israel" (Matthew 10:6). After His resurrection and then for another three-and-a-half years, His disciples preached mostly to Jews (Acts 1–6). After that second three-and-a-half-year period, in A.D. 34, the bold Stephen was brutally stoned by the Jewish Sanhedrin (Acts 7). This infamous deed marked the then-ruling Jewish leaders' final, official rejection of the gospel of our Savior.

Then the gospel went to the Gentiles. In Acts 9 Saul became Paul, the "apostle of the Gentiles" (Romans 11:13). In Acts 10, God gave Peter a vision revealing it was *now time* to preach to the Gentiles (Acts 10:1–28; see also Acts 13:46). Thus, approximately three-and-a-half years after the crucifixion—and at the end of the 70-week prophecy determined for the Jewish people—the gospel shifted to the Gentiles *exactly as predicted in Bible prophecy.*

The explosive evidence is overwhelming. Point by point, the events of Daniel's 70th week have been fulfilled in the past. These eight words found in Daniel 9:27 ("confirm," "covenant," "many," "midst," "sacrifice," "cease," "abominations," "desolate") all find perfect fulfillment in Jesus Christ and early Christian history. In the words of that 1846 Presbyterian publication:

> The *seventy weeks* of Daniel therefore, have certainly *ended* many centuries ago. We are not to look to the *future* for the fulfillment of these predictions. We must look to *the past*. And if to the past; where is there one who can have any adequate claims to being the subject of these prophecies, but *Jesus?* He, and he *only* can claim them; and to him they most certainly refer. [14]

> ... one would think, the people [the Jews] among whom [these events] occurred, could not possibly have misapplied the prophecy. [15]

But they did. In fact, one major reason the Jewish nation as a whole rejected its Messiah was because its scholars misinterpreted Daniel 9:27. They failed to see Jesus Christ as the predicted One who would die in the midst of the 70th week. Amazingly, the same thing is happening today. Sincere Christian scholars are now misapplying the very same prophecy.

The entire "seven-year period of Tribulation" theory is a massive mega-myth and may even go down in history as the Greatest Evangelical Misinterpretation of All Time. The whole concept is like a gigantic bubble. Once Daniel 9:27 is correctly understood and the sharply-pointed pin of truth is inserted, *pop goes the seven years*!

It's a fact: There is no text in the Bible that teaches a "seven-year Tribulation" at all. If you hunt for it, you will end up like the famous explorer Ponce de Leon, who tirelessly searched for the mystical Fountain of Youth but never found it.

The current debate and tremendous confusion over Pre-trib, Mid-trib, or Post-trib is really a smoke screen of the enemy to hide a much larger issue. What is that issue? We'll find out when we study closely what the book of Revelation *really teaches* about Israel, Babylon the Great, and Armageddon.

---

14 *Christ and Antichrist,* p. 49.

15 *Ibid.*, p. 47

— CHAPTER 7 —

Calvary and the Divine Divorce

He beheld the city and wept over it.
—Luke 19:41

> Then came Peter to him and said, 'Lord, how often shall my brother sin against me, and I forgive him? Up to seven times?' Jesus said to him, 'I do not say to you, up to seven times, but up to seventy times seven (Matthew 18:21–22, NKJV).

Christ's response to Peter's question is quite interesting. While He obviously was not saying that human forgiveness toward offenders should have a limit, "seventy times seven" equals 490— which just might have been a subtle reference to the 70-week prophecy of Daniel 9!

As we have seen, the 70-week period represented another opportunity for the chosen nation to demonstrate faithfulness to God. Israel's first temple had been destroyed and her children carried to Babylon because she had rejected God's warnings spoken through His prophets. Yet through divine love and mercy, another opportunity was granted to her "to finish the transgression, and to make an end of sins" (Daniel 9:24). Israel returned to her land and built a second temple.

Though Israel had sinned more than "seven times," God's forgiveness toward the nation was extended to "seventy times seven." Near the close of this period, One greater than the prophets would come. Then Israel's destiny *as a nation* would be determined by her response to God's Son.

Near the end of Jesus Christ's earthly life, He beheld Jerusalem "and wept over it, Saying, If thou hadst known, even thou, at least in this thy day, the things which belong unto thy peace! but now they are hid from thine eyes. For the days shall come upon thee, that thine enemies shall cast a trench about thee, and compass thee round, and keep thee in on every side, And shall lay thee even with the ground, and thy children within thee; and they shall not leave in thee one stone upon another; because thou knewest not the time of thy visitation" (Luke 19:41–44).

When Jesus spoke to Peter about forgiveness being extended "until seventy times seven," He knew the 70-week prophecy was soon to end. He also knew its awful significance to Israel as a nation, to Jerusalem, and to the second temple. Chapters 21–23 of Matthew reveal the sad, final, and explosive encounters between Jesus Christ and the leaders of His chosen people. It's now time to see the true meaning of those encounters.

During the week prior to His crucifixion Jesus "went into the temple of God, and cast out all them that sold and bought in the temple, and overthrew the tables of the moneychangers, and the seats of them that sold doves, And said unto them, It is written, My house shall be called the house of prayer; but ye have made it a den of thieves" (Matthew 21:12–13). At this point, Jesus still called the second temple "My house." But a change would come.

> Now in the morning as he returned into the city, he hungered. And when he saw a fig tree in the way, he came to it, and found nothing thereon, but leaves only, and said unto it, Let no fruit grow on thee henceforward for ever. And presently the fig tree withered away (verses 18–19).

Here the fig tree was a symbol of the Jewish nation. The "seventy times seven" countdown was nearing its close.

"And when he was come into the temple, the chief priests and the elders of the people came unto him as he was teaching" (verse 23). Their plan was to expose the humble Nazarene as a false Messiah and have Him put to death. Jesus told those leaders a parable that outlined the entire history of Israel in one panoramic sweep, culminating with their murderous designs:

> ... There was a certain householder [God], which planted a vineyard [Israel], and hedged it round about [God's love], and digged a winepress in it, and built a tower [the temple], and let it out to husbandmen [the Jewish leaders], and went into a far country: And when the time of the fruit drew near, he sent his servants [the prophets] to the husbandmen, that they might receive the fruits of it. And the husbandmen took his servants, and beat one, and killed another, and stoned another. Again, he sent other servants more than the first [continued mercy]: and they did unto them likewise. But *last of all* [notice the word,

> "last"] he sent unto them his son [near the close of "seventy times seven"], saying, They will reverence my son. But when the husbandmen saw the son, they said among themselves, This is the heir; come, let us kill him, and let us seize on his inheritance. And they caught him, and cast him out of the vineyard, and slew him [their final sin] (verses 33–39, italics added).

Jesus asked those leaders, "When the lord therefore of the vineyard cometh, what will he do unto those husbandmen? They said unto him, He will miserably destroy those wicked men, and will let out his vineyard unto other husbandmen, which shall render him the fruits in their seasons" (verses 40–41).

Did they realize what they were saying? Hardly! They had pronounced their own doom.

Looking His killers squarely in the eye, Jesus declared in words of burning truth, "Therefore I say unto you, The kingdom of God shall be taken from you, and given to a nation bringing forth the fruits thereof" (verse 43).

The Master Himself said it. The kingdom of God would be "taken" away from unbelieving Israel in the flesh and given to another "nation." Why? Because of their horrific sin of crucifying "the Son" (verses 38–39).

In His next parable, Jesus outlined the same historical sequence but added details of the destruction of Jerusalem and the call of the Gentiles.

> The kingdom of heaven is like unto a certain king, which made a marriage for his son, And sent forth his servants to call them that were bidden to the wedding: and they would not come. Again, he sent forth other servants, saying, Tell them which are bidden, Behold, I have prepared my dinner: my oxen and my fatlings are killed, and all things are ready: come unto the marriage. But they made light of it, and went their ways, one to his farm, another to his merchandise: And the remnant took his servants, and entreated them spitefully, and slew them. But when the king heard thereof, he was wroth: and he sent forth his armies, and destroyed those murderers, and burned up their city (Matthew 22:2–7).

This literally took place in A.D. 70 as Daniel's prophecy was fulfilled: "…the people of the prince that shall come shall destroy the city and the sanctuary …" (Daniel 9:26).

Continuing the parable, Jesus said, "Then saith he to his servants, The wedding is ready, but they which were bidden were not worthy. Go ye therefore into the highways, and as many as ye shall find, bid to the marriage" (Matthew 22:8– 9). Thus Christ represented the call of the Gentiles at the end of the "seventy weeks," which were specifically "determined" for the Jews.

"He came to His own, and His own received Him not" (John 1:11). Matthew 23 contains the Savior's final words of agony over Israel, His chosen nation. Eight times during His last public exchange with Israel's leaders, Jesus cried out, "Woe to you, scribes and Pharisees, hypocrites!" Finally, with a broken heart, the Son of the Infinite God declared: "O Jerusalem, Jerusalem, thou that killest the prophets, and stonest them which are sent to thee, how often would I have gathered thy children together, even as a hen gathereth her chickens under her wings, and ye would not! Behold, your house is left unto you desolate" (Matthew 23:37–38).

This time God was *not* saying, "You blew it. Let's try again." Israel's decision to crucify Christ would have permanent consequences. The result would be a searing separation—a painful, "Divine Divorce." As a Jewish Christian myself, I want to stress that the pain was on God's side. It was unbelieving Israel that *divorced herself* from Christ, her Faithful Lover—not vice versa.

Then "Jesus went out, and departed from the temple: and his disciples came to him for to shew him the buildings of the temple. And Jesus said unto them, See ye not all these things? verily I say unto you, There shall not be left here one stone upon another, that shall not be thrown down" (Matthew 24:1– 2). In A.D. 70, the second temple was destroyed by Romans and more than one million Jews perished. Such was the terrible results of that Divine Divorce.

Based on Daniel 9 and the teaching of our Messiah, we discover that the prophecy of "seventy times seven" represented the limits of national forgiveness for the Jewish *nation* (this doesn't apply to individuals). When Stephen was stoned by the Sanhedrin in A.D. 34, that moment was fraught with awful significance. It was so vital that Stephen, "being full of the Holy Spirit, gazed into heaven and saw the glory of God, and Jesus standing at the right hand of God." "Look!" the holy martyr cried. "I see the heavens opened and the Son of Man standing at the right hand of God!" (Acts 7:55–56, NKJV).

Jesus didn't "stand up" for no reason. A seismic shift was occurring. A new day was dawning. What would happen next?

It was time for the wall to come tumbling down.

— CHAPTER 8 —

When the Wall Tumbled Down

An invasion of armies can be resisted,
but not an idea whose time has come.
—Victor Hugo (1802–1885)

In 1989 the Berlin Wall came crashing down. Today there's nothing left of it. No longer is there a physical separation between East and West Germany; the two are one. According to the Bible, this is exactly what Jesus Christ—the Wall Breaker—accomplished for Jews and Gentiles. As it is written, "For he is our peace, who hath made both one, and has broken down the middle wall of partition between us" (Ephesians 2:14).

Solid New Testament truth is often quite different from what is taught in seminaries and discussed in theological circles. One of the biggest areas of confusion concerns Jews and Gentiles. Many have been taught that God has two separate plans—one for Jewish people, another for non-Jews. His plan for Gentiles is often applied to "The Church Age." This doctrine is a pillar of a system of theology called "Dispensationalism."

Notable Dispensationalist Charles Ryrie clarified, "The Church/Israel distinction is the *best* way to determine whether or not someone is a dispensationalist—the most important criterion." [16]

Additionally, "Dispensationalism has its roots in [J.N.] Darby's distinction between Israel and the Church." [17]

Yet we must inquire, *Does the New Testament really uphold this "Two-Plan Distinction?"*

First, let's back up a little. The ending of the "seventy times seven," those woes on the Pharisees, the transfer of the kingdom, the Divine Divorce, and the destruction of the second temple—

---

16 Charles C. Ryrie, *Dispensationalism Today* (Chicago, IL: Moody Press, 1965), pp. 44–5, 132, quoted in David MacPherson, *The Rapture Plot*, (Simpsonville, SC : Millennium III Publishers, 2000), p. 88.

17 Clarence Bass, *Backgrounds in Dispensationalism* (Grand Rapids, MI: Eerdmans, 1960), quoted in *The Rapture Plot*, p. 88.

none of this meant that *all* Israel had rejected its Messiah. Nor is it fair to categorically say, "The Jews killed Christ." No! This idea has horribly, unjustly, and cruelly fueled anti-Semitism for 2,000 years. It was not primarily "the Jews" who killed Christ, although there was a group of Jewish leaders who pressured the Roman governor, Pontius Pilate, to put Him to death. On a deeper level, it was really proud human nature resisting the humble One. It was your nature and mine. Jesus Christ died for "the sins of the whole world" (1 John 2:2).

Many Jewish people welcomed their Messiah. The 12 disciples were all Jewish. The Holy Spirit on the day of Pentecost fell only on Jews. It was 3,000 Jews who were then baptized (Acts 2:5, 22, 36, 41, 46). The early Church in Jerusalem was Jewish. Soon "a great company of the priests were obedient to the faith" (Acts 6:7). And apart from Luke, the entire New Testament was written by Jews.

The question must be asked, *Should we call this group of Jewish believers in Jerusalem "Israel" or "the Church"?* It's obvious they were both! Consider this: When Spirit-filled Stephen looked back at Israelite history, what did he call the Israel of Moses' time? He called it "the church in the wilderness" (Acts 7:38). Thus, according to Spirit-filled Stephen, Old Testament Israel *was* God's church!

As the early Jewish Church expanded into the Roman world, this question was finally raised: "Is our Messiah only for us? What about the Gentiles?" Then, unexpectedly, the Holy Ghost fell on non-Jews (Acts 10:44–45). Slowly, narrowness and prejudice broke down. A Jewish council of believers convened in Jerusalem to discuss the Jew-Gentile issue (see Acts 15). Finally, the Holy Spirit broke through the fog and revealed what was truly accomplished by the Messiah. A new day had dawned. The wall had come down. It was demolished by His cross.

Years later, Paul wrote this to believing Gentiles:

> Wherefore remember, that ye being in time past Gentiles in the flesh, who are called Uncircumcision by that which is called the Circumcision in the flesh made by hands; That at that time ye were without Christ, being aliens from the commonwealth of Israel, and strangers from the covenants of promise, having no hope, and without God in the world: But now in Christ Jesus ye who

> sometimes were far off are made nigh by the blood of Christ. For he is our peace, who hath made both one, and hath broken down the middle wall of partition between us ... to make in himself of twain one new man, so making peace; And that he might reconcile both unto God in one body by the cross ... (Ephesians 2:11–16).

Here Paul is quite clear. Believing non-Jews were *"in time past Gentiles* ... aliens from the commonwealth of Israel." But "now in Christ Jesus," Jews and Gentiles have become "one." *It's the truth.* So let's come out of the fog. The Wall Breaker has smashed "the middle wall of partition."

Paul was enraptured by this theme and wrote a lot about it.

> Whereby, when ye read, ye may understand my knowledge in the mystery of Christ which in other ages was not made known unto the sons of men, as it is now revealed unto his holy apostles and prophets by the Spirit; That the Gentiles should be fellowheirs, and of the same body (Ephesians 3:4–6).

Here Paul called this uniting of Jews and Gentiles into "the same body" the "mystery of Christ," which is "now" being revealed "by the Spirit." This mystery is more important than any mystery movie you might see. Again, Paul wrote, "There is neither Jew nor Greek, there is neither bond nor free, there is neither male nor female: for ye are all one in Christ Jesus" (Galatians 3:28). Pastors often say during marriage ceremonies, "What God has joined together, let no man separate!" This now applies to Jews and Gentiles in Jesus Christ.

According to the New Testament, believing Jews and believing Gentiles are now one. The two combined are "Abraham's seed" (Galatians 3:29). This is "the Israel of God" (Galatians 6:15, 16). This "mystery" has been accomplished by Jesus Christ's agony on Calvary. He did it. When He died, He broke down the wall. Now think about it. Should Christians gather bricks and rebuild the wall Jesus Christ died to abolish? Wouldn't this also be an "anti-Christ" thing to do?

What about Paul's controversial statement that "all Israel shall be saved"? (Romans 11:26). Many apply this to a mass conversion of Israelis at Armageddon. The context reveals otherwise. When Paul wrote that "all Israel shall be saved," he didn't mean that at some point every Jewish person would be saved. In the same chapter he wrote, "If by any means I may provoke to emulation them which are my flesh, and might save *some* of them" (verse 14, italics added). Again, in the same chapter, Paul declared "And they also, *if* they abide not still in unbelief, shall be grafted in" (verse 23, italics added). There's that tiny word "if" again.

"All Israel *shall* be saved," but as we studied earlier, the big question is, "Which Israel?" Remember, "They are not all Israel, which are of Israel" (Romans 9:6). There is an "Israel after the flesh" (1 Corinthians 10:18) and an "Israel of God" (Galatians 6:16) made up of Jewish people and Gentiles who believe in the Messiah. To apply "all Israel" which "shall be saved" to an end-time group of Jews or Israelis who are *separate from God's Church* is to deny the Wall Breaker's wonderful accomplishment on the cross.

Who is the "all Israel" in Romans 11:26? The answer is in the context. Paul wrote, "I speak to you Gentiles, inasmuch as I am the apostle of the Gentiles, I magnify mine office: If by any means I may provoke to emulation them which are my flesh, and might save some of them" (verses 13–14). Paul hoped that as the Gentiles responded to his preaching about the Messiah, that this would "provoke … some" of his Jewish brothers to re-examine the claims of Christ. Hopefully, this would lead "some" of them to believe in Jesus. Then this combined group of believing Jews and believing Gentiles would form the "all Israel" which "shall be saved."

Now for the entire context:

> For I would not, brethren, that you should be ignorant of this mystery, lest you should be wise in your own conceits; that blindness in part is happened to Israel, until the fullness of the Gentiles be come in. And so all Israel shall be saved: as it is written, There shall come out of [Zion] the Deliverer, and shall turn away ungodliness from Jacob: For this is my covenant unto them, when I shall take away their sins (Romans 11:25–27).

Notice: "The fullness of the Gentiles" is to "come <u>in</u>" (verse 25), *then* "all Israel" is saved (verse 26). Into *what* do they "come in"? Into "the good olive tree" (verse 24), which is Israel! Thus "all Israel" in verse 26 is a united group of believing Jews and Gentiles who have all responded to the Good News and "come in." To believe otherwise is to deny the context, reject "the mystery of Christ," and rebuild the wall Jesus Himself shattered on Calvary.

God thundered on Mount Sinai that "if" the Israelites obeyed His voice, "then" they would be "a peculiar treasure," a "kingdom of priests," and a "holy nation" (Exodus 19:5–6). In a letter to believers, Peter quoted these same words and applied them to God's Church:

> But ye are a chosen generation, a royal priesthood, an holy nation, a peculiar people… Which in time past were not a people, but are now the people of God (1 Peter 2:9–10).

In Old Testament days, God spoke about "Israel mine elect" (Isaiah 45:4). In New Testament times, Paul also called true believers in the Messiah—both Jews and Gentiles—"the elect of God" (Colossians 3:11–12).

Thus Peter and Paul agreed. They both quoted the exact words God spoke about Israel and applied them to believers in Christ.

They both taught that believing Jews and non-Jews together are "the people of God," "the elect of God," and "the Israel of God" (1 Peter 2:9–10; Colossians 3:11–12; Galatians 6:16).

The "two" are "one," and are "of the same body" (Ephesians 2:14–16; 3:6).

Through His cross, the Messiah Himself has performed this mysterious wedding ceremony. What God has joined together, let no man separate!

For those familiar with the term, this is not "Replacement Theology," which teaches that "the Church" has categorically "replaced" Israel. Neither is it "Separation Theology" (the opposite error of Dispensationalism), which teaches the unbiblical notion that Israel and God's Church are two distinct entities—and never the twain shall meet. Rather, this truth might be called an "Israel of God Theology" (Galatians 6:14–16) which sees God having one faithful Israel throughout history composed of true Jewish people and true Gentiles who believe in the Messiah (either looking forward to His cross in Old Testament days or looking back to His all-sufficient atonement). Biblically speaking, we should never exalt Jewish people (lest we build damnable pride in their hearts) or put them down (exhibiting deadly pride ourselves). Read Romans 11:17–23. Instead, we should realize we are all equal at the nail-pierced feet of the Crucified One. All of our sins put Him there. He loves us all.

Heavy fog on a highway can be dangerous. It often results in fatal car wrecks. As we shall soon see, if we don't come out of the fog of falsehood about Jews and Gentiles, we may crash at Armageddon.

— CHAPTER 9 —

1948: An Unsinkable Doctrine?

Truth is not determined by majority vote.
—Doug Gwyn

When the horrors of World War II were finally over and Hitler's Third Reich had come to an end, the world awoke to the nightmare of the German dictator's "Final Solution." Approximately six million innocent Jews had been brutally murdered. Public opinion then favored the return of the Jewish people to their ancient homeland.

The British controlled Palestine until May of 1948. On May 14, empowered by a resolution of the United Nations, the Zionist Movement proclaimed the rebirth of the State of Israel. For almost 2,000 years the Jewish people had been "wanderers among the nations." Now they were home. Yet their struggles had just begun.

An Arab League composed of Egyptians, Iraqis, Syrians, and Jordanians quickly invaded Palestine in an attempt to crush out the new nation. The fighting was heavy. Yet by 1949 the Arabs were defeated, and Israel was still in the land. In May of 1967, Egypt, Jordan, and Syria prepared for another attack. The Israelis struck first, and the war was over in six days. In 1973, at the beginning of the Jewish season of Yom Kippur, the Egyptians and Syrians attacked again. The battles were fierce and bloody. Yet by 1974, Israel was again on top and still in the land.

For the past 70 years, these astonishing events have gripped the attention of much of the Christian world. A firm conclusion has been reached by millions: what the world has witnessed is a direct fulfillment of Bible prophecy. This conviction is now being expressed on TV, radio, in books and magazines, at prophecy conferences, in Christian seminaries, and on the World Wide Web. The rebirth of the State of Israel in 1948 is now considered by countless Christians to be *the* most significant prophetic event of the 20th century.

Apocalyptic writer Randal Ross declared:

I call the establishment of the State of Israel "the ultimate prophecy time bomb," because when Israel became a legitimate state in the eyes of the world in May 1948, that single, seemingly isolated incident started the prophetic time clock ticking down toward the "zero hour" and the end of time. [18]

Best-selling evangelical author Hal Lindsey, whose blockbuster prophecy book, *The Late Great Planet Earth,* has sold over 28 million copies, dittoed:

> Since the restoration of Israel as a nation in 1948, we have lived in the most significant period of prophetic history. [19]

Still today, the majority of Christian beliefs about the end-times rest firmly upon this 1948 platform.

On April 10, 1912, the Titanic set sail from England for America. The largest ship in the world at that time, she was considered unsinkable. But after four days of smooth sailing, she hit the ice. Three hours later she was under water, on her way down to the bottom of the Atlantic Ocean. In many ways the 1948 theory is like the Titanic. In the minds of countless believers, it is considered unsinkable. However, in a few moments, this popular theory is going to hit the ice of God's Word. If it begins to sink, we should abandon ship as soon as possible.

There are three main arguments now being used to support the theory that Bible prophecy was fulfilled in 1948. Let's examine them.

1. The "Fig Tree" Argument:

In *The Late Great Planet Earth*, Hal Lindsey wrote:

> Jesus predicts an extremely important time clue. He says, 'Now learn a parable of the fig tree' [Matthew 24:32,–33 quoted] … The most important sign in Matthew has to be the restoration of the Jews to the land in the rebirth of Israel … When the Jewish people … became a nation again on 14 May 1948 the 'fig tree' put

18 Randall Ross, *The Next 7 Great Events of the Future* (Lake Mary, FL: Creation House, 1979), p. 23.

19 Hal Lindsay, *The Late Great Planet Earth* (Grand Rapids, MI: Zondervan Publishing House, 1970), p. 51.

forth its first leaves. Jesus said that this would indicate that He was 'at the door,' ready to return.[20]

Is this really what Jesus "said?" In a parallel passage, Luke records:

And he spake to them a parable; Behold the fig tree, and all the trees; When they now shoot forth, ye see and know of your own selves that summer is now nigh at hand. So likewise ye, when ye see these things come to pass, know ye that the kingdom of God is nigh at hand (Luke 21:29–31).

Because Luke wrote, "and all the trees; when they now shoot forth," we may clearly discern that Jesus did not have just one tree in mind representing Israel in 1948. In Matthew's gospel, Jesus explained His parable of the fig tree: "So likewise ye, when ye shall see all these things, know that it is near, even at the doors" (Matthew 24:34). When fig trees, and all trees, start blooming at the end of winter, we know summer is near. "So likewise," said Jesus, when we see "all these" various signs given in Matthew 24 occurring at the same time, then we may know His return is near. The fig tree is *not* the sign. It simply *represents* "all" the signs in Matthew 24, *none* of which is the specified rebirth of Israel in 1948. The ice of God's Word has just ripped the first hole in the bottom of the 1948 ship.

2. The "Israeli Victories" Argument:

Many view the Israeli victories in 1949, 1967, and 1973 as strong evidence that God had re-gathered Israel and was now fighting for His chosen nation, even though the leadership of that nation still does not believe in Messiah Jesus. Again, let's examine the argument.

First of all, "Jesus Christ is the same yesterday, today, and forever (Hebrews 13:8, NKJV). God says, "I am the Lord, I change not …" (Malachi 3:6). With this principle in mind, let's ask, Was God able to fight for Israel in the Old Testament when they were in unbelief?

After the Exodus, God promised to bring Israel into the Land of Canaan (Exodus 33:1–3). Twelve men were sent to spy out the territory. Yet after all the people heard the "evil report" about "the giants" in the land, they "murmured against Moses," saying, "let us return

20 *Ibid.*, p. 43

into Egypt" (Numbers 13:32–33; 14:2, 4). Then God pronounced this judgment: "But as for you, your carcasses, they shall fall in the wilderness. And your children shall wander in the wilderness forty years.... And ye shall know *my breach of promise*" (Numbers 14:32, 34, italics added).

Thus, because of Israel's unbelief, God was unable to fulfill His promise to that generation. This proves that God *can make a promise, but not fulfill it* to a certain group of people (see also 1 Samuel 2:30).

The ancient Israelites were unwilling to accept that 40-year sentence. The people proposed to go up anyway "to the place the Lord has promised" (Numbers 14:40). Moses said, "It shall not prosper. Go not up, for the Lord is not among you.... Therefore the Lord will not be with you.... But they presumed to go up.... Then the Amalekites came down ... and smote them" (Numbers 14:42–45).

This passage is full of instruction. Because of Israel's unbelief, God could not fight for her. Even though He promised, He wouldn't fulfill it. Years later, when Israel again "forsook the Lord ... they could not any longer stand before their enemies" (Judges 2:13–14). This truth is repeated many times in Joshua, Judges, Samuel, Kings, Chronicles, Jeremiah, etc.

Again, God does not change (Malachi 3:6). All throughout sacred history, He could not fight for Israel while they were in unbelief, thus He could not have been fighting for the Jewish nation in 1949, 1967, and 1973. Just because a nation wins battles is not evidence in itself that God is fighting for that nation.

Was God fighting for Hitler when he won so many battles? Was the Lord with the Nazis when they cruelly murdered six million Jews? Obviously not! Dear friend, the "Israeli Victory" argument is not based on a thorough study of the Word of God. Ice has just ripped a second hole in the hull of this "unsinkable" theory.

3. The End-Time Re-gathering Argument:

This is the big one. The idea is now being expressed all over the world that ancient prophecies which predicted a re-gathering of Israel back to their land were fulfilled in 1948. The main prophecy quoted is found in Ezekiel 36–38.

In Chapter 4 of *The Late Great Planet Earth,* Hal Lindsey gives the following three reasons why Ezekiel's prophecy must point to a 1948 fulfillment:

1. God said concerning Israel: "I will take you from among the heathen, and gather you out of all countries, and bring you into your own land" (Ezekiel 36:24).

2. The phrase, "out of all countries," must apply to "worldwide dispersion," and therefore cannot apply to the Babylonian captivity.

3. Ezekiel's prophecy will be fulfilled "in the latter days" (38:16) which supposedly is a "definite" phrase applying to "the time just preceding" the second coming of Jesus Christ. [21]

These reasons are accepted as unsinkable evidence of a 1948 fulfillment.

At first glance, Hal's arguments seem conclusive. But the following five responses not only cast doubt upon the three points just listed, but also prove that prophecy could *not* have been fulfilled in 1948.

1. God specifically told ancient Israel He would gather them "from all the nations" immediately "after seventy years be accomplished at Babylon" (Jeremiah 29:10, 14, 18). Thus an out of "all nations" gathering need not apply to the end-times.
2. The time period right after the Babylonian captivity was also called "the latter days" (Jeremiah 29:10–14; 30:24; 27:2–7; 48:47; 49:39; 50:1), thus this phrase is not always a "definite term" applying to "the time just preceding" Christ's return, as Hal Lindsey claims. Even Moses told ancient Israel, "I know that after my death … evil will befall you in the latter days …" (Deuteronomy 31:29).

3. Three times in Ezekiel 38, the re-gathered Israelites are described as a people who "dwell safely … dwelling without walls" (verses 8, 11, 14). These words "safely" and "without walls [of protection]" definitely do not apply to modern

21 *Ibid.*, pp. 49, 50

Israelis who now "dwell" amidst terrorists, who are often attacked by Islamic Jihadists, and who witness friends being blown apart by suicide bombers.

4. The reason Israel was scattered in Old Testament times was because she forsook God, broke His law, and disobeyed His word (Jeremiah 16:10–13; 29:18, 19). If you look carefully, according to the same Old Testament passages, Israel must *first* repent of her sins before such a re-gathering can be accomplished by God.

Here's the proof. God told Israel:

> It shall come to pass, when all these things are come upon thee, the blessing and the curse... and thou shalt call them to mind among all the nations, whither the Lord thy God hath driven thee, And shalt *return* unto the Lord thy God, and shalt obey his voice... *then* the Lord thy God will turn thy captivity... and will return and gather thee from all the nations... (Deuteronomy 30:1–3, italics added).

According to these inspired words, when God scatters Israel among "all the nations," if she returns and obeys His voice, *then* He will re-gather her. If she doesn't return and obey, then this prophecy *cannot* be fulfilled by God. Because the Messiah has come, this "return to the Lord" must include embracing Jesus Christ. The facts of history reveal that Jewish Zionism did not meet this spiritual condition in 1948.

Again, God told ancient Israel, "*If* ye transgress, I will scatter you abroad among the nations: But *if* ye turn unto me... *yet* will I gather them ..." (Nehemiah 1:8–9, italics added).

> And ye shall seek me, and find me, when ye shall search for me with all your heart. And I will be found of you, saith the Lord: and I will turn away your captivity, and I will gather you from all the nations (Jeremiah 29:13–14).

These Scriptures are plain. Israel must first repent, *then* God will gather her. Once again, this condition was not met by the Zionist movement in 1948. The "unsinkable" theory is starting to go down. "Lower the lifeboats!" is the cry from heaven!

Even Ezekiel 36 contains conditional elements. Notice carefully, "Thus saith the Lord God. In the day that I shall have cleansed you from all your iniquities I will also cause you to dwell in the cities, and the wastes shall be builded" (Ezekiel 36:33).

Thus, "in the day" God cleanses Israel from "all" of her sins, in that day He would "also cause" her to dwell in her cities. This did not happen in 1948. Israel as a nation was not cleansed from "all" her iniquities at that time—especially had it not forsaken its Heaven-confronting sin of rejecting the Son (Matthew 21:37–39).

Jonah predicted, "Yet forty days, and Nineveh shall be overthrown" (Jonah 3:4). Yet 40 days later, Nineveh remained unscratched. Why? Because the prophecy was conditional. Nineveh repented, so God's judgment was deferred. The same conditional elements are also found in the re-gathering prophecies. Because Israel did not first repent and return to the Lord Jesus Christ, the promises of re-gathering could not have been fulfilled by God in 1948.

5. Ezekiel declared: "And the word of the Lord came unto me, saying, Son of man, set thy face against Gog, the land of Magog ..." (38:1–2) "In the latter years thou shalt come into the land that is brought back from the sword, and is gathered out of many people ..." (verse 8). "Thou shalt ascend and come ..." (verse 9) "Upon the people that are gathered out of the nations ..." (verse 12) "And it shall come to pass at the same time when Gog shall come against the land of Israel, saith the Lord God, that my fury shall come up in my face" (verse 18). "I will rain upon him, and upon his bands, and upon the many people that are with him, an overflowing rain, and great hailstones, fire, and brimstone.... And they shall know that I am the Lord" (verses 22, 23).

Chapter 5 of *The Late Great Planet Earth* is called "Russia Is a Gog." There Hal Lindsey applied the Ezekiel 38 prophecy to 1948 and then to a final Middle East conflict between Russia and Israel. Yet the explosive truth is that the book of Revelation actually applies

Ezekiel's prophecy to a global event predicted to occur at the end of the millennium.

Earlier we discovered how Matthew took Hosea 11:1, which originally applied to Israel, and then declared it "fulfilled" in Jesus Christ (Matthew 2:15). We also saw how Paul made a similar Old Testament to New Testament application when he applied "the seed of Abraham," which was definitely "Israel," to "one… which is Christ" (Isaiah 41:8; Galatians 3:16). Amazingly, Revelation 20 does the same thing with Ezekiel 38:

> And when the thousand years are expired, Satan shall be loosed out of his prison, And shall go out to deceive the nations which are in the four quarters of the earth, Gog and Magog, to gather them together to battle: the number of whom is as the sand of the sea. And they went up on the breadth of the earth, and compassed the camp of the saints about, and the beloved city: and fire came down from God out of heaven, and devoured them (Revelation 20:7–9).

The major elements are the same. Both Ezekiel 38 and Revelation 20 speak about Gog, Magog, a great army, a final gathering for battle against Jerusalem, and fire from heaven. Yet Revelation 20 applies these things to the end of the millennium, to a global Gog and Magog, and to a final global battle against the saints and the beloved city, which is the New Jerusalem (Revelation 3:12; 21:10; Hebrews 12:22). Thus Revelation 20 takes what originally applied to Israel and *applies it to a final global battle against the saints of Jesus Christ who are inside the New Jerusalem at the end of the millennium.*

Why does Revelation do this? For the same reason we discussed earlier. So the "word of God" won't be made of "none effect" in spite of the unbelief of some natural Jews (see Romans 9:6). God did promise in Ezekiel 38 (and in Zechariah 14) that He would defend Israel and Jerusalem during a final battle. And He will. He will defend His Israel in the Spirit which will dwell inside the New Jerusalem at the end of the millennium. According to Revelation 20, this is how Ezekiel 38 will be fulfilled. The big question is: *Are we willing to accept the New Testament's application of Old Testament prophecies?* If not, we are not being faithful to "the *whole* counsel of God" (Acts 20:27, italics added).

On April 15, 1912, at 2:20 a.m., the unsinkable Titanic was fully underwater. A third of her passengers sat shivering in lifeboats, yet the majority were corpses plunging lifelessly through dark waters toward the bottom of the Atlantic Ocean. How about us? Will we abandon the "1948 Ship" before we get into serious trouble? Our Captain is pleading, "Get into the lifeboats!" If we refuse, we may sink down to the bottom of the sea.

— CHAPTER 10 —

When the Euphrates Runs Dry

If the Apocalyptic Israel were proved not to be the literal Israel, there is not a Futurist but would admit that their cause was lost.
—Edward B. Elliott (1793–1875)[22]

We have reached the heart of this book. It is finally time to study the last book in the Book: Revelation. As we open its sacred pages we discover statements about "mount Zion" (14:1, NKJV), "the twelve tribes of Israel" (7:4–8), "Jerusalem" (21:10), "the temple" (11:19), "Sodom and Egypt" (11:8), "Babylon" (17:5), "Gog and Magog" (20:8), "the great river Euphrates" (16:12), and "Armageddon" (16:16). Thus it is obvious that Revelation uses the terminology and geography of the Middle East in its prophecies.

What is happening right now all over Planet Earth is that evangelical scholars are applying most of these terms literally—to those literal places, and to the Jewish nation in the Middle East. Here is the explosive question: Does our Lord intend for these prophecies to be literally applied to "Israel after the flesh" (1 Corinthians 10:18), or should they be applied to "the Israel of God" (Galatians 6:16) in Jesus Christ?

To discover the answer, the beginning is the best place to start. The very first sentence of God's last book calls it, "The Revelation of Jesus Christ" (Revelation 1:1). Thus Jesus Himself is Revelation's Source, Center, and Interpreter. This will become immensely significant soon. Beyond this, in chapter one, John was "in the Spirit" when he received his vision (verse 10). So the entire book was originally seen by John through Spirit-enlightened eyes, not flesh-vision. A key lesson is: We also need our eyes illuminated by the Holy Spirit in order to interpret Revelation's message correctly.

John beheld the Risen One walking "in the midst of the seven golden candlesticks" (verses 12 and 13). The idea of "seven golden candlesticks" takes our minds back to the seven-branched candlestick inside the Jewish temple before it was destroyed in A.D. 70 by Roman

22 E. B. Elliott, *Horae Apocalypticae*, Vol. 4, Fifth Edition (1862), p. 609.

armies. Yet in Revelation, the "seven golden candlesticks" are not literal, but clearly symbolic. What do they represent? Explaining "the mystery," the Risen Interpreter declared, "The seven candlesticks which you saw *are the seven churches*" (Revelation 1:20, italics added). Thus, in Revelation's very first chapter, Jesus took something extremely Jewish and used it *symbolically to represent His Church.* As we shall see, this is one of the key interpretive principles to understanding the entire book.

In Revelation 2, in a dictated letter to "the church in Thyatira" (verse 18), Jesus reproved His people for allowing "that woman Jezebel, who calls herself a prophetess, to teach and to seduce my servants …" (verse 20). Jezebel was a wicked woman in Old Testament times that entered Israel and caused problems. Was Jesus saying "Jezebel" had been reincarnated, or resurrected, and was literally teaching deception within Thyatira? Obviously not. A little reflection reveals He used the word "Jezebel" as a *symbol* of an evil movement that was affecting His Church. As with the seven golden candlesticks, God's Messiah took something from Jewish history and applied it to His Church, "the Israel of God" (Galatians 6:16).

In Revelation 3 the Heavenly Interpreter dictated another letter to "the church in Philadelphia" (verse 7) in which He said a Christian could become "a pillar in the temple of My God," and have a place "in the city of My God, which is New Jerusalem" (verse 12). Don't miss the significance of this. Not only did Jesus again use Jewish imagery—the temple—and apply it symbolically to His Church, but He also identified another city, "the New Jerusalem," as God's headquarters. And this city will not be a remodeled earthly Jerusalem with its bullet holes covered and the blood of suicide bombers scrubbed away. This one "comes down out of heaven" (verse 12).

What about Revelation's prophecy of the river Euphrates drying up before Armageddon? The Word says, "The sixth angel poured out his vial upon the great river Euphrates; and the water thereof was dried up, that the way of the kings of the east might be prepared." (Revelation 16:12). Does this apply to the literal river Euphrates flowing near Baghdad, which our American troops crossed in Operation Iraqi Freedom, or is something more intended?

Hal Lindsey applies the prophecy of Revelation 16:12 to "a vast Oriental army" and a future "war in the Middle East." He wrote:

> The Euphrates has presented a formidable problem for the corps of engineers of many ancient armies of the past. In this future invasion, however, God Himself will see to it that the river is dried up so that a trap is set for triggering the last great war of mankind.[23]

When Hal Lindsey (and countless others) read about the Euphrates drying up, they interpret this literally. The "kings of the east" are often assumed to be Chinese kings or warriors whose foot soldiers will someday cross a dry riverbed before attacking Israel at Armageddon. This is how Revelation 16:12 is expected to be fulfilled, yet we cannot help but wonder: Why would an Asian country ever launch such an army against Jerusalem? And if one did attack Israel, why would its leaders first send its army *so far north* to cross the Euphrates? Why not plan a more direct attack, send planes, launch missiles, or drop bombs?

I am about to prove that such Middle East literalism fails to grasp the true meaning and genius of the book of Revelation. It fails to discern that Revelation is simply using Old Testament terms, history, and geography as symbols—just like Jesus did when He mentioned "Jezebel"—that are meant to be applied in a special, spiritual sense. As noted earlier, on August 9, 1945, the United States government finally decided to drop an atomic bomb called the "Fat Man" upon Nagasaki. It is now time to drop our version of the "Fat Man" upon the globally popular—yet wrong—Middle East Method of interpreting Bible prophecy.

"The sixth angel poured out his vial upon the great river Euphrates; and the water was dried up, that the way of the kings of the east might be prepared" (Revelation 16:12, NKJV). In order to understand this prophecy, we must first study some ancient Bible history about Israel and Babylon. In 605 B.C., Babylon conquered Jerusalem and took the Jews captive for 70 years (Daniel 9:2). After these 70 years, an amazing set of circumstances occurred. The Euphrates dried up, Babylon was conquered from the east, and Israel was delivered. As we shall see, this forms the background for a true understanding of Revelation 16:12.

23 *The Late Great Planet Earth*, pp. 70, 71.

Ancient Babylon sat on the river Euphrates (Jeremiah 51:63–64). A wall surrounded the city. The river Euphrates ran through Babylon, entering and exiting through two spiked gates with bars that reached down to the riverbed. When these double doors were shut and all other entrances were closed, Babylon was impregnable. Yet she was to fall suddenly and be destroyed (Jeremiah 51:8). Then God would call Israel, saying, "My people, go out of the midst of her" (Jeremiah 51:45). As we shall soon see, these exact words are repeated in Revelation to God's spiritual Israel about the importance of coming out of Mystery Babylon (Revelation 17:4–5; 18:2–8).

In 538 B.C., on the night of ancient Babylon's fall, her king and subjects were drunk with wine (Daniel 5). So were the guards, and they forgot to fully close the double doors. Over 100 years earlier, God had predicted concerning Babylon and the Euphrates, "I will dry up thy rivers" (Isaiah 44:27). The Lord also spoke about a man named "Cyrus," who conquered Babylon, saying, "I will… open before him the two leaved gates; and the gates shall not be shut" (Isaiah 45:1). Moreover God called Cyrus "My shepherd" and "His anointed" (Isaiah 44:28; 45:1). Thus Cyrus was a type of Jesus Christ. And he came "from the east"! (Isaiah 46:11).

Inside the British Museum in London lies the famous Cyrus Cylinder, and it describes how Cyrus conquered Babylon. Cyrus and his army dug trenches upstream alongside the river Euphrates. By diverting the water, the river slowly went down as it ran through the city of Babylon. No one noticed. At night, at the height of Belshazzar's drunken feast, the water became low enough for Cyrus and his men to quietly sneak under the double doors, which had been left open. Quickly they overran the doomed city, killed the king (Daniel 5:30), and conquered Babylon. Then Cyrus issued a decree to let Israel go (Ezra 1).

Revelation uses the events, geography, and terminology of the Old Testament and applies them universally to Jesus Christ, the Israel of God, and spiritual Babylon at the end of time. A failure to discern this principle has resulted in a widespread misunderstanding of Revelation, a mistaken Middle-East focus, and massive *end time delusions.*

In Revelation 17 a shiny angel said to John, "Come, I will show you the judgment of the great harlot who sits upon many waters.… So he carried me away in the Spirit into the wilderness. And I saw a woman sitting on a scarlet beast which was full of names of blasphemy … having in her hand a golden cup … And on her forehead a name was written, MYSTERY, BABYLON THE GREAT, THE MOTHER OF HARLOTS …" (Revelation 17:1, 3–5, NKJV).

Just like in chapter one of Revelation, John was again "in the Spirit" when he beheld this Satanic Seducer. Even so must we be "in the Spirit" in order to understand what this Apocalyptic Prostitute is really all about.

John saw this Harlot sitting "upon many waters," just like ancient Babylon sat upon the Euphrates river. Yet in Revelation, these "many waters" do not refer to the literal river Euphrates which today trickles amidst bombed-out Iraqi buildings. No! Revelation's angel interpreter said, "The waters which you saw, where the whore sits, are peoples, multitudes, nations, and tongues" (Revelation 17:15, NKJV).

The genius of Revelation is that it uses the history of the Old Testament and then applies it spiritually to a Mystery Babylon, which now sits upon the "many waters" of a spiritual river Euphrates. According to the angelic interpreter, this river of "many waters" actually *represents* "peoples, multitudes, nations and tongues" around the world that support the Harlot and her global deceptions (Revelation 17:15; 18:23). Echoing the ancient words of Jeremiah yet applying them spiritually and globally, Revelation says, "Babylon is fallen, is fallen, that great city, because she made all nations drink of the wine of the wrath of her fornication." Revelation 14:8).

The error of those who adopt the Literal Middle East Method of interpretation stems from:

1. The belief that these prophecies must apply to the Israel of the flesh
2. A failure to study the Old Testament's root history behind Revelation's prophecies
3. A failure to apply that history spiritually and universally to the Israel in the Holy Spirit
4. A failure to center Revelation entirely in Jesus Christ and His warfare against His global enemies.

Modern interpreters usually apply the words "Babylon," "Euphrates," and "kings of the east" to a literal city, a literal river, and literal Middle Eastern armies attacking literal Jews. Yet Revelation speaks of that "which *spiritually* is called Sodom and Egypt," about a "*Mystery* Babylon," and about "many waters" that *represent* "peoples, multitudes, nations, and tongues." Revelation 11:8; 17:1, 5, 15, italics added).

In 1887, one of England's greatest Protestant prophecy teachers, H. Grattan Guinness, insightfully wrote:

> Futurism is literalism, and literalism in the interpretation of symbols is a denial of their symbolic character. It is an abuse and degradation of the prophetic word, and a destruction of its influence. It substitutes the imaginary for the real, the grotesque and monstrous for the sober and reasonable. [24]

This issue can be compared to the wearing of two different pairs of glasses. If we put on the "literal Middle East glasses" we will "see" Revelation's prophecies as applying only to literal places and to literal Israel after the flesh. But if we put on the "Middle East symbolism glasses" and read Revelation through the Holy Spirit's aid, we will "see" these prophecies applying to the Israel of God in Jesus Christ. Paul wrote to Christians, "But ye are not in the flesh, but in the Spirit." (Romans 8:9). If we put on the wrong glasses and interpret prophecy according to the flesh, we will end up blinder than a bat in daylight. But if we put on the right glasses and interpret prophecy through the enlightenment of the Holy Ghost, then we will say, "I was blind, now I see" (John 9:25).

A woman in prophecy represents a church. The true Church of Jesus Christ is called "His wife," who makes "herself ready" for the marriage supper of the Lamb (Revelation 19:7–8). What about the false woman so graphically described in Revelation 17? Hold onto your seat. In a few moments I will prove—as Protestants have done for centuries—that the Babylonian Whore represents a false form of Christianity that leads "peoples, multitudes, nations and tongues" away from the pure truth of Heaven's Lamb. She is the net result of a historical "falling away," which Paul plainly predicted in

24 Henry Grattan Guinness, *Romanism and the Reformation* (1887), p. 163. (Reprinted by Hartland Publications in 1995.)

2 Thessalonians 2:3–4. As Guinness revealed, "The contrast is between Church and Church; the faithful Church and the apostate Church."[25]

Specifically, Hell's Harlot has these identifiable characteristics:

1. She is a "Mother" (Revelation 17:5).
2. She has harlot daughters (Revelation 17:5).
3. She sits on "seven mountains" (Revelation 17:9).
4. Her colors are "purple and scarlet" (Revelation 17:4).
5. She is extremely wealthy with lots of "gold" (Revelation 17:4).
6. She is "drunk with the blood of the saints" (Revelation 17:6).
7. She is a "great city" (Revelation 17:18).
8. She has ruled "over the kings of the earth" (Revelation 17:18).
9. She intoxicates "all nations" with her "wine" (Revelation 14:8).
10. Many of God's own people are still inside of her (Revelation 18:4).

Best-selling evangelical author Dave Hunt, whose 20-plus books have combined sales of over 3,000,000 copies, has tackled this topic head-on in his penetrating book, *A Woman Rides the Beast: The Roman Catholic Church and the Last Days*. Chapter titles include: "Mystery, Babylon," "A City on Seven Hills," "Blood of Martyrs," "Dominion over Kings," "What about Mary?" "Sacrifice of the Mass," and "The Reformation Betrayed." Marshaling a vast amount of evidence from Scripture, history, and the Protestant Reformation, Hunt concludes, "The leaders of the Reformation were certain that she [the Revelation 17 harlot] represented the Roman Catholic Church. …"[26]

With a pen dipped in concern for both Protestants (who have lost their knowledge of history) and bewildered Roman Catholics, Mr. Hunt reveals that an apostate form of "Christianity will take over the world … not real Christianity but an Antichrist counterfeit

25 *Ibid.*, p. 88

26 Dave Hunt, *A Woman Rides the Beast: The Roman Catholic Church and the Last Days* (Eugene, OR: Harvest House Publishers, 1994), p. 14.

thereof."[27] I agree wholeheartedly with Mr. Hunt on the identity of the Hell's Harlot, yet we disagree on the role of Israel in prophecy.

During the first Persian Gulf war (1990–1991) Saddam Hussein made a feeble attempt to begin rebuilding the ancient city of Babylon whose ruins now lie about 50 miles south of Baghdad. When he did, prophecy books came pouring off Christian presses declaring, "Look! Bible Prophecy is being fulfilled. Babylon is rising!"

At the exact same time, John Elson's article, "Apocalypse Now?" appeared on the last page of the February 11, 1991, issue of *TIME* magazine. Elson insightfully commented, "The temptation to seek clues to the Second Coming on CNN is easy to understand, since Saddam Hussein has proclaimed himself a successor to Nebuchadnezzar, the Babylonian king who enslaved the Israelites of old. That makes it deceptively easy for prophecy mongers to identify Iraq with Babylon. Somewhat awkwardly, *it also undercuts a long standing Protestant tradition that this symbol of corruption refers to the Church of Rome.*"[28] Amazing!

Israel and the End of the World supports the historic Protestant view, not futuristic, Dispensationalist fables. Along with Luther, Calvin, Wesley, Spurgeon, Wylie, Hunt, and countless others, we also realize the "Woman" who "rides the beast" symbolizes "the Church of Rome." No other church fits every specification of the prophecy, nor does any other *organization* for that matter. Chillingly, the Roman Church even calls herself "Holy Mother Church," "The mother and teacher of all the churches."[29] Prophecy calls her "the Mother of Harlots" (Revelation 17:5).

H. Grattan Guinness offers this hard-to-refute summary:

> Now, in conclusion, read this wonderful prophecy concerning "Babylon the Great" *in the clear and all-revealing light of history.* I ask those of you who have read the history of the last eighteen centuries, did not Rome Christian become a harlot? Did not Papal Rome ally itself with the kings of the earth? Did it not glory itself to be as a queen, and call itself the Mistress of the World? Did it

27 *Ibid.*, p. 45

28 John Elson, "Apocalypse Now?" *TIME*, February 11, 1991, p. 88 (italics added).

29 Rev. Peter Geiermann, C. SS. R, *The Convert's Catechism of Catholic Doctrine* (St. Louis, MO: B. Herder Book Co., 1946), pp. 102, 103.

> not ride upon the body of the beast, or fourth empire, and govern its actions for centuries? Did not Papal Rome array itself with gold and precious stones and pearls? Is not this its attire still? We appeal to facts. Go to the churches and see. Look at the priests; look at the cardinals; look at the popes; look at the purple robes they wear; look at the scarlet robes; look at the encrusted jewels; look at the luxurious palaces in which they live; look at the eleven thousand halls and chambers in the Vatican, and the unbounded wealth and glory gathered there; look at the glorious spectacles in St. Peter's at Rome, casting even the magnificence of royalty into the shade. Go and see these things, or read the testimony of those who have seen them. Shamelessly Rome wears the very raiment, the very hues and colors, portrayed on the pages of inspired prophecy. You may know the harlot by her attire, as certainly as by the name upon her brow.[30]

Mystery Babylon is called "the Mother of Harlots." But wait a minute! Think carefully. A "Mother" must have children. Prophecy says the Lady in Red is actually a Mother of "*Harlots*." That tiny "s" at the end of the word reveals that the Mother Church has *harlot daughters*. If the "Mother" refers to a church, then a little reflection reveals that her daughters must also refer to churches and organizations that, while claiming separation from Rome, nevertheless teach fundamental doctrines that really originate with Mom. Solemn thought![31]

Further proof that the Mother and Daughters represent, as Dave Hunt states, "not real Christianity but an Antichrist counterfeit thereof," comes from the fact before King Jesus Christ returns in the clouds, God calls *His own people* to leave Babylon's infernal grip. "And I heard another voice from heaven, saying, 'Come out of her, My people, lest you share in her sins, and lest you receive of her plagues'" (Revelation 18:4).

In the Old Testament, when Cyrus dried up the literal Euphrates, this exact same call was given by God to literal Jews urging them to

30 *Romanism and the Reformation*, pp. 89, 90.

31 To learn more about the role of the Roman Catholic Church in end-time prophecy, see the author's larger book, *End Time Delusions,* now available from White Horse Media.

come out of literal Babylon. "My people," the Lord pleaded through Jeremiah, "go out of the midst of her, and deliver every man his soul from the fierce anger of the Lord" (Jeremiah 51:45). This exact same call is issued in Revelation to sincere Christians who are inside spiritual Babylon. Now don't miss this point. If Babylon in Revelation is a *spiritual* Babylon, then the Israel that is called out must be a *spiritual* Israel. We must all come out lest we "share in her sins" (Revelation 18:4, NKJV).

"Come out of her, My people" (Revelation 18:4), says the Lord. Thus God considers many of His own people to be still inside of Mystery Babylon. This must refer to large numbers—both Protestant and Catholic—of real Christians who are serving the Lord to the best of their ability. This must also apply to many who are even now teaching false prophecy. Yet God still calls them "My people" because He knows their hearts. God mercifully still sees them as part of His spiritual Israel. But they are confused! In fact, "Babylon" means "confusion." Because of today's global religious confusion, especially about Bible prophecy, millions of the Lord's people now believe false illusions about Babylon and Israel. Yet according to Revelation 18:4, Jesus Christ is now calling us all to "come out" of spiritual confusion and into the full truth of His Word. We must leave Babylon before it's too late. Why? Because soon its river will run dry.

"The sixth angel poured out his vial upon the great river Euphrates; and the water thereof was dried up" (Revelation 16:12). "Babylon the Great" sits on "the great river Euphrates." According to God's angel, the river now represents "peoples, multitudes, nations, and tongues" (Revelation 17:15) around the world who, refusing to come out, continue to support the false doctrines of Mystery Babylon. Soon "the sixth angel" will pour out "his vial upon the great river Euphrates." This vial is one of the seven "vials of the wrath of God" (Revelation 16:1). Thus, it is *the wrath of God*—not Turkey or some other Middle East nation—that will dry up the Euphrates.

What does this mean? Brace yourself. It means that God's wrath will eventually be poured out upon *people* around the world who choose to support Mystery Babylon's deceptions all the way until the end!

When the "peoples, multitudes, nations, and tongues" that have resisted the Holy Spirit's truth-arrows and have chosen to support

The Mistress of Temptation all the way to the end finally experience God's burning wrath, their spiritual blinders will be ripped from their eyes. They will realize they've been duped—big time. What loving conviction failed to accomplish, God's justice finally will. They will turn on their teachers, preachers, and priests with madness and fury. What a horrific nightmare! They will "hate the whore, and shall make her desolate and naked, and shall eat her flesh, and burn her with fire" (Revelation 17:16). Their support for the Scarlet Harlot will vanish. This is how Babylon's water will dry up, preparing the way for the "kings of the east" (Revelation 16:12).

Cyrus came from "the east" to conquer ancient Babylon (Isaiah 44:26–28; 46:11). The word "east" literally means, "sun rising." The name "Cyrus" means "sun." Cyrus was a type of Jesus Christ, "the Sun of righteousness" (Malachi 4:2). In Revelation, God's holy angels come from the east (Revelation 7:2). Jesus said, "As the lightning cometh out of the east, and shineth even unto the west; so shall also the coming of the Son of man be" (Matthew 24:27).

Jesus Christ is coming from the east with the armies of heaven as "KING OF KINGS, AND LORD OF LORDS" (Revelation 19:14, 16). Thus, the "kings of the east" are not Asian hordes, Chinese legions, Russian armies, or Islamic Jihadist warriors, but King Jesus and His armies which will soon descend from the eastern skies to conquer Babylon and deliver Israel at Armageddon!

But which Israel will Jesus deliver? It will surely be an Israel in the Spirit who, having chosen to walk in the Spirit and to interpret prophecy according to the Spirit, has also chosen to "come out" of Mystery Babylon and to forsake its fleshy ways (Galatians 5:16, 25; Revelation 18:4).

Let's be part of *that* Israel.

— CHAPTER 11 —

Frogs, Fables, and Armageddon

Truth is the only safe ground to stand on.
—Elizabeth Cady Stanton (1815–1902)

Most people don't like frogs, but I loved to catch them when I was a boy. Did you know the book of Revelation talks about frogs? Amazingly, it connects them with the battle of Armageddon. John wrote:

> I saw three unclean spirits like frogs come out of the mouth of the dragon, and out of the mouth of the beast, and out of the mouth of the false prophet. For they are the spirits of devils, working miracles, which go forth unto the kings of the earth and of the whole world, to gather them to the battle of that great day of God Almighty … And he gathered them together into a place called in the Hebrew tongue Armageddon (Revelation 16:13–14, 16).

The dragon, the beast and the false prophet represent the three parts of Mystery Babylon (verse 19). A careful reading of Revelation 16:13–16 plainly reveals that Armageddon involves a final global battle between the dragon, the beast, the false prophet, the three frog-like spirits, the kings of the whole world and God Almighty.

Once again, symbolism is involved here. The "dragon" is earlier said to have seven heads and ten horns (Revelation 12:3), as does "the beast" (Revelation 13:1). The "false prophet"—the third member of this unholy trinity—is also referred to as "another beast" with "two horns like a lamb" but which speaks as a dragon (Revelation 13:11). Three frog-like spirits eventually speak to the entire world through the lips of these three deceivers. Clearly this involves massive, global *end time delusions*. The "dragon" is primarily a symbol of Satan himself (Revelation 12:9).

According to Protestant historicists like H. Grattan Guinness and countless others, "the beast" symbolizes the Papal power.[32]

32 See the author's larger book on this subject, *End Time Delusions.*

What about the "false prophet"? Think about it. What comes from false prophets anyway? *False prophecy.* Therefore, while this may not be the full meaning of the text, Revelation's highly symbolic prophecy about a frog-like spirit speaking globally through the lips of a false prophet surely represents God's warning about a false system of prophetic interpretation that is now deceiving millions with false ideas about the beast itself, Babylon, Israel and Armageddon.

A plague of frogs was one of the 10 plagues of Egypt. "Aaron stretched out his hand over the waters of Egypt; and the frogs came up, and covered the land of Egypt" (Exodus 8:6). This forms the background for Revelation 16:13. In the Old Testament, the frogs came up from "the waters of Egypt." In Revelation 16:12–13, the three frog-like spirits come from "the great river Euphrates," whose waters represent the "peoples, multitudes, nations and tongues" that support the Harlot (Revelation 17:15).. The third frog-like spirit speaking globally through the lips of the false prophet involves a gigantic system of false prophecy that even now "covers the land." In contrast to the lies of all three frogs is Heaven's counter-message of the three angels, which tell the truth "to every nation, tribe, tongue, and people" (see Revelation 14:6–12). Study carefully: It's the Three Frogs versus the Three Angels.

The third frog of false prophecy is now teaching a secret Rapture at the beginning of a 7-year Tribulation, a future Antichrist, a literal drying up of a literal Euphrates, and a literal Middle East Armageddon involving literal armies attacking literal Jews. Dear friend, *this is all false prophecy.* It is part of "the wine" of Babylon, which deceives all nations (Revelation 14:8; 18:23).

In the New Testament, Jesus used the phrase "new wine" to represent His pure teaching while "old wine" symbolized the false doctrines of the Pharisees (see Luke 5:36–39). Wine confuses the mind. In Revelation, the "wine of Babylon" represents the tantalizing potion of *end time delusions* with which Babylon confuses and dupes the world.

Much of this wine concerns Israel. That's one reason why the Harlot is called a counterfeit "Mystery." She denies "the mystery of Christ" we read about earlier. She has rebuilt a wall between Jews and Gentiles—a wall Jesus Christ smashed at the cross (Ephesians 2:14–17).

Paul plainly predicted that the time would come when the majority would "turn away their ears from the truth, and shall be turned unto fables" (2 Timothy 4:3–4). The clock has struck twelve. We are now living in the time of frogs and fables.

Have you read the fable of a handsome prince who was turned into a frog? What a disaster! Yet this frog-prince still had the power of speech. One day the unfortunate frog-prince happened to meet a stunningly beautiful princess. He opened his mouth, spoke, and convinced the maiden to kiss him. Presto! The frog became a prince again.

The moral of this story for us today is that if we ourselves have unwittingly fallen under the subtle influence of frogs and fables, it's high time to return to the Prince. We need the kiss of royalty. The Holy Bible says, "Kiss the Son. …" (Psalm 2:12). Through the words of truth that fall from the lips of the Truth Teller, we can be delivered from the third frog of false prophecy.

"And he gathered them together into a place called in the Hebrew tongue Armageddon" (Revelation 16:16). This is the only time the exact word *Armageddon* is used in the Bible. The truth is, there is no literal place called "Armageddon" anywhere in the world. This mysterious word is a combination of two words: *Ar*, which means "mountain," and *mageddon*, reminiscent of the ancient valley of Megiddo (see 2 Chronicles 35:22). In the Old Testament, Megiddo was a place of bloody battles and great slaughters. In fact, many scholars suggest the literal meaning of *Megiddo* is "slaughter" or "cut off." Thus the mysterious word, *Armageddon*, could literally mean a "mountain" of "slaughter" upon which God's enemies are "cut off."

In Daniel 2, a "mountain" is definitely used symbolically to refer to God's global kingdom which will one day "fill the whole earth" (Daniel 2:35, 44–45). In Revelation 16:14 we read about a global gathering of "the kings of the earth and of the whole world" to the final battle. These worldwide forces of Satan compose his global kingdom. They will all be gathered to "Armageddon," to the Mountain of Slaughter. We conclude that "Armageddon" refers to a worldwide battle in which Satan's global kingdom will finally be "cut off" by the approaching kingdom of God Almighty.

The actual slaughter of Satan's global kingdom is described immediately after the word "Armageddon" is used. Read it for yourself:

> And he gathered them together into a place called in the Hebrew tongue Armageddon. And the seventh angel poured out his vial into the air; and there came a great voice out of the temple of heaven, from the throne, saying, It is done. And there were voices, and thunders, and lightnings; and there was a great earthquake, such as was not since men were upon the earth, so mighty an earthquake, and so great. And the great city was divided into three parts, and the cities of the nations fell: and great Babylon came in remembrance before God, to give unto her the cup of the wine of the fierceness of his wrath. And every island fled away, and the mountains were not found (Revelation 16:16–20).

Contrary to the all-pervasive teaching of the third frog, these words clearly describe divine wrath upon *spiritual* Babylon and a *global* slaughter that reaches far beyond the Middle East.

Prior to Armageddon, the three frog-like spirits "go forth unto the kings of the earth and of the whole world, to gather them to the battle of that great day of God Almighty" (Revelation 16:14). John wrote in a parallel passage, "I saw the beast, and the kings of the earth, and their armies, *gathered together* to make war against Him who sat on the horse, and against His army" (Revelation 19:19, italics added). Who is the gathering at Armageddon really against? Literal Jews? No! It is a gathering of the world forces of Mystery Babylon against the Holy Warrior on a white horse and against His army. That Warrior is King Jesus Himself (see Revelation 19:11–16).

What about His army? Who will compose His holy battalion? It will be an army of "legions of angels" (Matthew 26:53) who return with King Jesus at His second coming (Matthew 16:27; 24:31).

The following passage describes the actual battle of Armageddon, the victory of King Jesus, the doom of Hell's Mistress, and the final slaughter of all "nations" who have been duped by Lucifer's lying legionnaires. Read it reverently with a humble heart:

> Now I saw heaven opened, and behold, a white horse. And He who sat on him was called Faithful and True, and in righteousness He judges and makes war. His eyes were like a flame of fire, and on His head were many crowns. He had a name written that no one knew except Himself. He was clothed with a robe dipped in blood: and His name is called The Word of God. And the armies

in heaven, clothed in fine linen, white and clean, followed Him on white horses. Now out of His mouth goes a sharp sword, that with it He should strike the nations. And He Himself will rule them with a rod of iron. He Himself treads the winepress of the fierceness and wrath of Almighty God. And He has on His robe and on His thigh a name written: KING OF KINGS, AND LORD OF LORDS (Revelation 19:11–16, NKJV).

On the fateful morning of September 11, 2001, Steve Miller was inside the fully intact South Tower of the World Trade Center in New York City, just minutes after the North Tower burst into flames. As he and his associates descended from the 80th floor, he paused on the 55th floor to use the men's room. It was shortly after 9:00 am.

Shall I phone my wife? he pondered.

Suddenly a voice echoed over the PA system: "Don't panic. The building is safe. Return to your offices."

As Mr. Miller glanced sideways at the flaming building right next door and saw people jumping from windows a thousand feet above the ground, his innate distrust of official voices won out. He made a bolt for the stairs just as a second plane exploded into the South Tower a few floors above him. He ran outside, and as he hurried across the bridge toward Brooklyn, he looked back just in time to see his building vanish in a cloud of smoke. Upon his arrival at home he fell into his teary-eyed wife's arms.

"Oh, my God," she cried. "I thought you were dead."

As we near "the battle of the great day of God Almighty" (Revelation 16:14), my earnest appeal to you is this: Don't trust *every* official-sounding Evangelical, Dispensationalist or Roman Catholic voice you hear, or you may end up dead. There are times when we must go against the grain, in the opposite direction of the crowd. Sincere prophecy teachers who now focus on literal Israel and earthly Jerusalem may say, "Don't panic. Our theories are safe. Stay in the building." But the fact is, someday these twin towers of prophetic error will be totally vaporized.

In spite of Revelation's description of a global slaughter, the bottom-line message of Armageddon is actually good news! Heaven's encouragement: The world forces of Satan's kingdom will one day come crashing down. So take heart! The Rider on the white horse—

whose name is Faithful and True—will conquer. "The meek shall inherit the earth; and shall delight themselves in the abundance of peace" (Psalm 37:11).

God's love shall endure forever, and some day "there shall be no more death, nor sorrow, nor crying. There shall be no more pain, for the former things have passed away. Then He who sat upon the throne said, 'Behold, I make all things new.' And He said to me, 'Write, for these words are true and faithful" (Revelation 21:4–5, NKJV).

In the midst of Armageddon's ruins will lay the third frog of false prophecy. That frog will never become a prince. But we can! As Steve Miller fell into the arms of his worried wife, why not fall right now into the loving arms of Jesus Christ and let His abundant mercy kiss new life into your soul.

Let's forsake all frogs and fables as we follow the King.

— CHAPTER 12 —

Thunder from Heaven's Temple

Moses didn't come done from Mount Sinai with Ten Suggestions, but with Ten Commandments.
—Author unknown

> He gathered them together into a place called in the Hebrew tongue Armageddon. And the seventh angel poured out his vial into the air; and there came a great voice out of the temple of heaven, from the throne, saying, It is done. And there were voices, and thunders, and lightnings; and there was a great earthquake. … (Revelation 16:16–18).

Immediately after Armageddon is mentioned, the next verse focuses on "the temple of heaven." There are voices, thunder, lightning, and a great earthquake. God is definitely trying to get our attention! His thunderous message is, "Look to the Heavenly Temple!"

The third frog wants us to gaze in the opposite direction, toward a supposed-to-be-rebuilt third temple on earth. It's a basic diversion strategy. In 1991, during the Persian Gulf War and Operation Desert Storm, the allies built up their forces just east of Iraq in the Persian Gulf. Saddam Hussein then thought an attack was coming from the east, but the allies attacked from the west. This attack was successful because Saddam was not looking in that direction. Today, the third frog is doing the same thing. He wants us to look in the wrong direction and expect a rebuilt future third temple inside Jerusalem on earth. If we follow his croaking counsel, we will fail to discern life-saving truths that come from another direction.

Again John wrote, "The temple of God was opened in heaven, and there was seen in his temple the ark of his testament: and there were lightnings, and voices, and thunderings, and an earthquake. …" (Revelation 11:19). Here we see the same manifestations of God's power we just read about in Revelation 16. Yet now these fireworks are connected with the seeing of "the ark" in heaven's temple. Millions have seen the movie *Raiders of the Lost Ark*. In it, Indiana Jones finds the lost Ark of the Covenant. That movie is fantasy, while Revelation is reality. As a result of the third frog's subtle strategy of diversion, the knowledge of the heavenly ark has been lost. But prophecy says that knowledge is to be regained and His ark will be "seen" by those who discover this truth.

The same manifestations of God's power described in Revelation also occurred when the Almighty came down on Mount Sinai to give the Ten Commandments (Exodus 19:16–18; 20:1–17). The Ten Commandments are called "tables of testimony, tables of stone, written with the finger of God" (Exodus 31:18). After Moses received the stone tables, he "came down from the mount, and put the tables in the ark" (Deuteronomy 10:5). Because those two tablets were placed inside the ark, that special box was called "the ark of the testimony" (Exodus 40:20–21).

Revelation 11:19 says, "The temple of God was opened in heaven, and there was seen in his temple the ark of his testament. …" Inside that ark are the original Ten Commandments. Here is the truth God wants us to see. Yet the devil is determined to blind us, and this is the reason for his diversion strategy. Through the third frog of false prophecy, the enemy seeks to divert our minds toward a rebuilt third temple on earth. Why? Because that temple has no ark! If we follow his croaking counsel, we will look in the wrong direction, bypass heaven's temple, and fail to discern the end-time significance of the Holy Law of God.

Mystery Babylon has not only rebuilt a wall between Jews and Gentiles, she also often teaches that the Ten Commandments were given only for Israel, not the Church. But Jesus Christ, the Founder of the Church, boldly testified:

> Think not that I am come to destroy the law, or the prophets: I am not come to destroy, but to fulfill. For verily I say unto you, Till heaven and earth pass, one jot or one tittle shall in no wise pass from the law, till all be fulfilled. Whosoever therefore shall break one of these least commandments, and shall teach men so, he shall be called the least in the kingdom of heaven: but whosoever shall do and teach them, the same shall be called great in the kingdom of heaven (Matthew 5:17–19).

Did you catch that? Here the Master Teacher said we should "do" and "teach" the "commandments," and not even "break one" of them!

A few verses later, Jesus specifically quoted the seventh commandment: "You shall not commit adultery" (Matthew 5:27). Then the Pure One expounded upon that, saying, "Whoever looks on a woman to lust after her has committed adultery with her already in his heart" (verse 28). Here Jesus revealed the spiritual depth of the seventh commandment, and He also applied it to "whoever," meaning everyone throughout the world. In a time of exploding internet pornography, the massive proliferation of Adult DVDs, Hollywood sex scandals, flesh-flaunting TV programs and marital unfaithfulness, how we need this commandment!

Jesus also rebuked some tricky Pharisees for their slick way of weaseling around God's fifth commandment, which states, "Honor your father and your mother" (Matthew 15:4). Christ declared, "Thus have ye made the commandment of God of none effect by your tradition" (Matthew 15:6). In an age when children often rebel against mom and dad, and when the lyrics of one rock song even tell kids to "Kill Your Parents," how we need God's Law!

If you look carefully, Jesus Christ and the New Testament fully uphold every one of the Ten Commandments originally stated in Exodus 20. Pick up your Bible and read for yourself:

1. Put God first (Matthew 4:10)
2. Avoid idols (1 John 5:21; Revelation 22:15)
3. Respect God's name (Romans 2:24)
4. Keep the original[33] seventh-day Sabbath holy (Matthew 12:12; Luke 23:56)
5. Honor your parents (Matthew 15:4; Ephesians 6:1–3)
6. Don't murder (Matthew 19:18; 1 John 3:15)
7. Don't commit adultery (Matthew 5:27–28; Galatians 5:19)
8. Don't steal (Mark 7:22; Ephesians 4:28)
9. Don't lie (Romans 13:9; Revelation 21:8)

33 See the author's pocketbook, *Discovering the Lost Sabbath Truth.*

10. Don't covet (Luke 12:15; 1 Corinthians 6:12)

It's a fact: Jesus Christ upheld the Big Ten and rebuked others for breaking them. Yet today, many professed Christians pit Christ against the Ten Commandments, even though Jesus specifically said, "*Do not think* that I came to destroy the Law. . . ." (Matthew 5:17, italics added).

Are they really referring to the Jesus of the New Testament? We might as well ask, "Will the real Jesus please stand up?" The Ten Commandments are unchangeable, that's why God inscribed them with His own Almighty finger on solid rock. Have you heard the expression, "We can change this or that, for it's not written in stone"? This illustration stems from the Ten Commandments. In other words, what's on stone can't be altered.

James wrote to Christians:

> Whosoever shall keep the whole law, and yet offend in one point, he is guilty of all. For he that said, Do not commit adultery, said also, Do not kill. Now if you commit no adultery, yet if thou kill, thou art become a transgressor of the law (James 2:10–11).

Think about it. How can a New Testament Christian "become a transgressor of the law" if the law doesn't exist anymore? Can a speeding driver receive a ticket for transgressing a speed law that isn't there? Of course not! Speed laws do exist. And if we will but slow down and read carefully the words of Jesus Christ and of James, we will discover that the Ten Commandments remain and apply to Christians.

Paul is clear that Christians are not saved by the law, but by the grace of Jesus Christ. "For by grace are ye saved through faith, and this not of yourselves, it is the gift of God" (Ephesians 2:8). Again, we are "justified by faith without the deeds of the law" (Romans 3:28). Yet Paul is equally clear that the Big Ten remain and have a purpose. What is this purpose? Paul declared, "By the law is the knowledge of sin" (Romans 3:20). "I had not known sin, but by the law" (Romans 7:7). "That sin through the commandment might become exceedingly sinful" (Romans 7:13, NKJV). The law makes sin rise before our faces so it becomes "exceedingly sinful" to our astonished eyes. Especially is this true when we realize God wrote Ten *Commandments*, not Ten *suggestions*.

The law is like a mirror. When people crawl out of bed in the morning and look in the mirror, they often dislike what they see. Yet the mirror is important. We *need* to look at it. It is the same with God's law. If we have the courage to look, we may not like what we see, but this uncomfortable revelation will help us to feel our need for Jesus Christ's cleansing blood. "Wherefore the law was our schoolmaster to bring us unto Christ, that we might be justified by faith" (Galatians 3:24).

The good news is, "Christ died for our sins" (1 Corinthians 15:3). What are "our sins"? Heaven's answer is, "Sin is the transgression of the law" (1 John 3:4). When we look at God's law we see our sins and discern what slew our Savior.

Two thousand years ago, outside Jerusalem on a hill called Calvary, Heaven's innocent Lamb became guilty. He experienced our sins of breaking the Ten Commandments. "Our sins" entered His mind and pierced His heart. He felt the sword of God's wrath (see Zechariah 13:7)—the full execution of His justice against transgression.

Moved by unfathomable love and pity, Jesus took our death sentence. He paid the full price for breaking God's Law. It's the truth. Jesus Christ died on Mount Calvary because the entire human family (starting with Adam and Eve) has broken the Ten Commandments proclaimed on Mount Sinai. The evangelical book, *Revival's Golden Key*, by Ray Comfort with Kirk Cameron, correctly upholds the present authority of the Ten Commandments for Christians today while showing its proper relationship to the grace of our Lord and Savior Jesus Christ.[34]

Just to clarify, God gave another law on Mount Sinai that concerned His earthly temple and the dripping blood of sacrificial animals. That law involved "Sacrifice and offering, burnt offerings and offerings for sin" (Hebrews 10:1, 8). Paul said it was this very "[sacrificial] law of commandments contained in ordinances" that formed "the middle wall of partition" between Jews and Gentiles (Ephesians 2:14–16). When Jesus died, He "caused the sacrifice ... to

34 Ray Comfort with Kirk Cameron, *Revival's Golden Key* (Gainesville, FL: Bridge-Logos Publishers, 2002).

cease." (Daniel 9:27). He took that law of sacrifices, and "nailed it to the cross" (Colossians 2:14).

But that abolished law was not the Ten Commandments. The Big Ten are eternal, were written on solid rock, and are now inside the heavenly ark (Revelation 11:19). Modern "Babylon," which means "confusion," has not only rebuilt a wall between Jews and Gentiles, but it has also mistakenly nailed the *wrong law* to the cross.

"God is not the author of confusion" (1 Corinthians 14:33). In order to overcome the tricks of Revelation's Scarlet Temptress, we must accept the words of Jesus Christ (Matthew 5:17–19), of Paul (Romans 3:19–20; 7:7, 12–13), of James (James 2:10–12), and of John (1 John 3:4) regarding the perpetuation of the Ten Commandments. We must look square into the Big Ten and realize we're doomed without Christ's grace and blood. Losing all self-confidence, we must repent of our sins and trust fully in the merits and worthiness of our Savior. Then we have the promise of full forgiveness for all of our sins.

"If we confess our sins, he is faithful and just to forgive us our sins, and to cleanse us from all unrighteousness" (1 John 1:9). The Lamb Himself will wash us from all filthiness "in His own blood" (Revelation 1:5) and clothe us with "white garments" (Revelation 3:18, NKJV), the white robes of His own spotless righteousness (Revelation 7:9). Through the power of the Holy Spirit—now that we have a fresh start—we shall be supernaturally enabled to obey God's Law (Romans 8:4). Jesus Himself said, "If you love me, keep my commandments" (John 14:15). He was quoting the second commandment (compare with Exodus 20:6).

This brings us to the heart of the great divide that will ultimately separate God's Israel in the Spirit from the flesh-ways of the Scarlet Harlot. It's a moral issue regarding love for Jesus Christ practically demonstrated by the Spirit-filled keeping of the Ten Commandments now housed in heaven's ark. In Revelation, this issue is symbolically represented as being shouted to the whole world as with a megaphone by an angel, specifically by one called "the third angel." "And the third angel followed them, saying with a loud voice… Here is the patience of the saints: here are they that keep the commandments of God and the faith of Jesus" (Revelation 14:9, 12). This exact issue is repeated in Revelation 12:17 and 22:14. It will be understood by all who avoid the third frog's diversion strategy, who look to the right temple, and whose Spirit-enlightened eyes discern the heavenly ark (Revelation 11:19).

The true "Israel of God" (Galatians 6:16) will focus on "the temple of God" (Revelation 11:19) and will keep "the commandments of God" (Revelation 14:12) by "the Spirit of God" (Romans 8:9, 14) as it journeys toward what our Lord and Savior Jesus Christ called "the city of my God . . . the New Jerusalem" (Revelation 3:12).

Don't let the *third* frog lead you from the *third* angel to an imaginary future *third* temple that has no ark.

— CHAPTER 13 —

144,000 Israelites Indeed

We can easily forgive a child who is afraid of the dark.
The real tragedy of life is when men are afraid of the light.
—Attributed to Plato (427–347 B.C.)

"The dragon was wroth with the woman, and went to make war with the remnant of her seed, which keep the commandments of God, and have the testimony of Jesus Christ" (Revelation 12:17). "Here is the patience of the saints: here are they that keep the commandments of God, and the faith of Jesus" (Revelation 14:12). Just as a "remnant" of ancient Israel came out of literal Babylon and rebuilt a second temple (Haggai 1:12), even so will a final "remnant" of spiritual Israel come out of spiritual Babylon to keep the Ten Commandments now housed safely inside the ark in heaven's temple (Revelation 11:19).

God's final remnant is referred to in prophecy as the 144,000 (Revelation 14:1–5). They are described as coming from "all the tribes of the children of Israel" (Revelation 7:4). Does this mean they are all literal Jews? Millions think so. Some popular teachers liken this group to 144,000 Jewish Billy Grahams who will evangelize the world during the Tribulation after the Rapture. But is this right? We have previously seen that Paul wrote that Jews and Gentiles are now "one" and are part of "the same body" through Jesus Christ (Ephesians 2:14; 3:4–6). Does the last book in the Bible contradict Paul's words? Does Revelation rebuild a wall between Jews and Gentiles that Jesus Christ abolished at the cross? Of course not!

Let's put on our "New Testament Spirit-glasses" and take a closer look. The 144,000 are described as standing on "Mount Zion" with the Lamb (Revelation 14:1, NKJV). In the Old Testament, Mount Zion is where Jerusalem sat. Yet in Revelation, "Mount Zion" does not refer to any mountain in the Middle East.

John wrote, "And he carried me away in the Spirit to a great and high mountain, and shewed me that great city, the holy Jerusalem, descending out of heaven from God" (Revelation 21:10). As John was "in the Spirit," even so must we be "in the Spirit" in order to see the truth about Mount Zion and the 144,000. Paul told believers, "But you have come to Mount Zion, and to the city of the living God, the heavenly Jerusalem… to the general assembly and church of the firstborn, who are registered in heaven. …" (Hebrews 12:22, 23). Thus there is a heavenly Mount Zion on which the New Jerusalem sits. It is the home of the Church.

This is where John saw the 144,000.

In the New Testament, James wrote his letter "to the twelve tribes which are scattered abroad" (James 1:1). Who were these twelve tribes? In the next sentence James called them, "My brethren." Then he wrote to them about "the trying of [their] faith" (James 1:3). Thus, these "twelve tribes," which James wrote to as a unit, were believers in Christ. In the same letter he counseled those from among these "twelve tribes" who were sick to "call for the elders of the church" for special prayer (James 5:14). Thus to James, the "twelve tribes" were definitely part of the Church.

The 144,000 "follow the Lamb wherever He goes" (Revelation 14:1, 4, NKJV). Therefore they are Christians who love Jesus. They are "not defiled with women; for they are virgins" (Revelation 14:4). This does not mean the 144,000 is composed of only literal, Jewish, unmarried or celibate men. No. If so, this would be teaching mass celibacy, a dogma which Paul called a "doctrine of devils" (1 Timothy 4:1–3). In 2 Corinthians 11:2, Paul also used the word "virgin," and he applied it to the Church. What about the 144,000 not being "defiled with women"? This is talking about the Harlot Ladies of Revelation 17.

The atomic truth is that the 144,000 represent a final remnant of God's Israel in the Spirit, composed of believing Jews and Gentiles, who are not "defiled" by the deceptions and false prophecies of the Mother and Daughters of Mystery Babylon (Revelation 17:5). The reason Revelation refers to them as coming from "all the tribes of the children of Israel" is because, in the process of exiting modern Babylon, all deception, and even from their own besetting sins, they have gone through a similar "wrestling experience" with the Lord as did Jacob when his name was changed to Israel (Genesis 32:24–28).

Earlier we learned that the name "Jacob" literally meant "crook" or "deceiver." This name was an accurate description of Jacob's character. He purposefully lied to Isaac three times (Genesis 27:19–24) and then stole his father's final blessing from his older brother Esau. As a result of his wicked deception, Jacob went into exile for 20 years. On his way back home, Jacob discovered Esau was coming with 400 men to meet him (Genesis 32:6). Filled with guilt, shame, and terror, Jacob feared his life would be snuffed out because of his sin.

Then came that lonely night of wrestling with the Angel of God. Finally, just before dawn, Jacob gave up on himself, repented of his sin, and firmly gripped the heavenly Messenger, saying, "I will not let you go, unless you bless me" (Genesis 32:26). Then came this response from the Angel: "Your name shall be called no more Jacob, but Israel: for as a prince you have struggled with God and with men, and have prevailed" (verse 28). Through repentance, self-renunciation, humility, and faith, Jacob overcame his naturally deceptive nature. God gave him a new heart, a new name, a new character. He had gained the victory.

That very experience that transformed Jacob into a "spiritual Israel" is a type of the transforming experience that will produce the 144,000. This is a deep thought, yet it's true. This insight is more significant than the rediscovery of the Titanic's sunken hull. And it applies to us. By nature we are all like Jacob—sinful, crooked, and deceptive. Maybe, while reading this book, you have discovered the shocking truth that you yourself have unwittingly deceived others about Bible prophecy. The thought is terrifying!

The Bible says, "A false witness shall not be unpunished, and he that speaketh lies shall not escape" (Proverbs 19:5). Just as Esau was coming to meet Jacob, even so does Bible prophecy predict that God Almighty will eventually come to punish Mystery Babylon for her lies (Revelation 18:8). All who "love and make a lie" will unexpectedly find themselves outside the New Jerusalem (Revelation 22:15). "All liars" will be hurled into the lake of fire (Revelation 21:8). Thus Truth vs. Lies is a Life vs. Death matter.

Yet Jesus Christ loves us all. On a cruel cross He agonized, suffered, bled, and died for all of our sins, including our sins of deception. He rose from the dead and ascended to heaven. And now, as our merciful High Priest standing before the ark in Heaven's temple, Jesus Christ has given us the book of Revelation to teach us the truth. At this very moment, the Good Shepherd is pleading with us to leave the tricks of

Mystery Babylon before it's too late. "Come out of her, my people," is His final call from heaven (Revelation 18:4, 8). Soon modern Babylon will be "utterly burned with fire: for strong is the Lord God who judgeth her" (Revelation 18:8). She'll be pulverized.

This is now our night for spiritual wrestling. Soon the darkness will end. It was at the breaking of the day when the heavenly Messenger finally touched Jacob's thigh (Genesis 32:24–25). It was then that Jacob's self-confidence was finally broken as He clung for dear life to the Angel of God. So it may be with us. According to prophecy, we are even now at "the breaking of the day." Jesus Christ is coming soon! Oh, may the Master touch us now and break us! May the Holy Spirit explode every ounce of wicked pride that so often pulsates within our sin-clogged veins. Following the example of Jacob, let's cling to Jesus Christ for our very lives and say, "I will not let You go, unless You bless me."

As with Jacob, if we humble ourselves, repent of our sins, and depend entirely upon God's mercy, the King of Israel will not forsake us. If in simple faith we cling to Jesus Christ, He will forgive us, change us, and give us a new name. By faith we can hear the Master say, "Your name shall no longer be called Jacob, but Israel: for as a prince you have struggled with God and with men, and have prevailed" (Genesis 32:28, NKJV). Jesus is the true Seed of Abraham. He is the Victorious One. Through faith in Him, God will cause "us to triumph in Christ" (2 Corinthians. 2:14). Through the Truth-teller, we can escape the distortions of Mystery Babylon. Through God's boundless grace, we can each become, like Jacob, a spiritual Israel.

The Bible specifically says about the 144,000, "In their mouth was found no guile [deception]: for they are without fault before the throne of God" (Revelation 14:5). Like Nathanael, they are "Israelite[s] indeed, in whom is no guile" (John 1:47). They overcome Hell's Harlot, her deceptions, and her false prophecies. The 144,000 are like Jacob. They prevail over their own deceptive natures through the grace of Heaven's Lamb.

The above passage in Revelation 14:5 about the 144,000 finds its root in the Old Testament. "The remnant of Israel shall not do iniquity, nor speak lies; neither shall a deceitful tongue be found in their mouth" (Zephaniah 3:13). Thus the final remnant of Israel will be made up of people who speak the truth. They must be one with Jesus Christ, who is "the Truth" (John 14:6). They must also be guided by "the Spirit of Truth" (John 16:13). Composed of Jews and Gentiles who believe in the Messiah, they will be God's final Israel in the Spirit. It is my personal opinion that the number "144,000" is symbolic. Yet whether literal or symbolic, I hope we will all "be in that number, when the saints go marching in."

This volatile book can be compared to a heat-seeking missile whose purpose is to explode prophetic falsehood. As it flies on its mission, its intention is not to promote anti-Semitism against Jewish people, or to offend sincere Bible-believing Christians. Rather, its goal is to illuminate minds and save souls. At this very moment, the Christian Church is filled with gigantic misinterpretations of prophecy—about Daniel's 70th week, the identity of Babylon, Israel, and the Ten Commandments—which are out of harmony with the true teaching of Jesus Christ and the New Testament. Seismic transformations must occur within churches, prophetic ministries, seminaries, websites, and YouTube channels. In order for this to happen, God's missile must hit some big targets!

If you have been led to believe all Christians will disappear with a "poof!" before an end-time seven-year period of Tribulation hits, this lie must be unmasked. If you have been taught that Revelation's statements about Jerusalem, Mount Zion, the temple, Gog, Magog, Sodom, Egypt, Babylon, and the Euphrates River apply to those literal places in the Middle East, these errors must be shattered. If well-meaning people have convinced you that Armageddon's major contestants are Russia, China, Iran, or Muslim radicals like Hamas or Hezbollah against the Jewish State, then someone must lock this error into sight within an instrument panel and push a glowing red button reading, "Launch Missile Now." It's time to flee from all frogs and fables.

Every one of these supposedly unsinkable theories will hit the ice at Armageddon. They will all sink just like the Titanic. "Abandon ship!" is the cry from our Captain. "Come out of her, my people" is the plea of our soon-coming Deliverer (Revelation 18:4). Instead of looking toward an earthly Jerusalem south of Haifa and east of Tel Aviv, our focus should be "the holy city, New Jerusalem" which will someday "come down out of heaven from God" (Revelation 21:2).

Rather than dwelling on the Wailing Wall or Temple Mount, our vision should center on "the sanctuary" in heaven, "the true tabernacle" (Hebrews 8:1–2) where our faithful High Priest now ministers His crimson blood in our behalf. Jesus is the Seed of Abraham, the true Israel (Isaiah 41:8; Galatians 3:16). "And if you belong to Christ, then you are Abraham's seed, and heirs according to the promise" (Galatians 3:29). Never forget these words.

May God help us all to be among Revelation's final remnant of Israel in the Spirit of whom it is written, "Here is the patience of the saints: here are they that keep the commandments of God, and the faith of Jesus" (Revelation 14:12). According to the Lord's "sure word of prophecy" (2 Peter 1:19), such a commandment-keeping remnant will exist right before the return of Jesus Christ on a "white cloud" (Revelation 14:14–16). They will be ready for the descent of the Son of Man with His "sharp sickle" (verse 14) and will have an eternal home inside the New Jerusalem (Revelation 21:9–27).

Charing Cross is the name of a subway station in London. I'm told there is a cross there, serving as a reference point for travelers. A small child once lost her way in the big city and sat down on a street corner, crying.

"What's wrong little girl?" asked a passing police man.

"I'm lost! I can't find my way home," the girl sobbed.

Willing to drive her home himself, the man asked for her address. She didn't know. The name of her street? No idea. Her phone number? "I can't remember!" the lost girl moaned through her tears.

Frustrated, the police man finally asked, "Little girl, what *do* you know?" After thinking for a moment, the child's face lit up. "Mister, I know how to get home from the cross. If you can just take me to the cross, I can find my home from there!"

Dear friend, it's the same for us. We must all come to the cross—Dispensationalists, Protestants, Catholics, Jewish people, Arabs, Muslims, atheists, rock 'n rollers, and everyone else. We can find our way home from there. As we journey towards the New Jerusalem, our Friend Jesus has made every provision that we shall arrive safely. He loves us, points out our dangers, reproves, convicts, and purifies (see Daniel 12:10). Thank the Lord, He has given us "the Spirit of truth" and His "sure word of prophecy" to guide us on the narrow road (John 16:13; 2 Peter 1:19; Matthew 7:13–14)

May Paul's words apply to us: "But you are not in the flesh, but in the Spirit" (Romans 8:9). Let's live in the Spirit *and interpret prophecy according to the Spirit.* Through the love, mercy, kindness, and unfathomable grace of Jesus Christ, may each of us receive courage and strength to become "an Israelite indeed, in whom is no guile" (John 1:47).

In these final days of darkness before the bursting forth of eternal day, it is my earnest prayer that God will use *Israel and the End of the World* to strike, penetrate, explode—and illuminate—some very big targets.

www.peacefinders.org

Your Gateway to finding peace with God

Bible Study with Us

Peacefinders offers a variety of Bible study options, including mail-in, online, and a variety of tools and study resources to help you get the most out of your personal Bible study and grow your faith.

Free Inspirational Books

We offer an entire library of Christian classics and other Bible-based reading for you and your family at no cost or obligation. Some of the best devotional and teaching materials available.

Inspirational Christian Media

We have put together a selection of music, video, podcasts, and other inspirational media to enrich your spiritual life and help you stay focused on what is good, true, noble, and pure.

Essentials for Christian Living

Our Father in Heaven wants us to be healthy and happy— health and happy homes, marriages, minds, bodies, and a wholesome picture of reality. We have put together some fantastic resources to help you find and fulfill your God-given purpose and in life.

a Lifeline in Crisis

Here you will find an extensive list of helpful resources to help when you or your loved ones need guidance and support as you face some of life's most difficult challenges.

MORE BOOKS ABOUT BIBLE PROPHECY AND GLOBAL END-TIME DELUSIONS

BY STEVE WOHLBERG

GOD'S FINAL WARNING: THE THREE ANGELS' MESSAGES

As millions focus on the Middle East as the center of last day events they are missing God's final message to the world represented by three mighty angels warning about the Judgment, Babylon, the Beast, its deadly Mark, and the return of Jesus Christ (see Revelation 14:6-16). Discover what most prophecy teachers aren't telling you!

THE TRUTH ABOUT THE SABBATH: PROOF THAT THE SEVENTH DAY (SATURDAY) IS STILL GOD'S HOLY DAY

The first angels' message of Revelation 14:6,7 urges humanity to "worship Him that made heaven, and earth, and the sea, and the fountains of waters,"—which is an exact quote from Exodus 20:8-11 about the seventh-day Sabbath. Discover what the Bible and Jesus Christ taught about the Sabbath, and how Sunday as a day of worship came into Christianity from the Catholic Church.

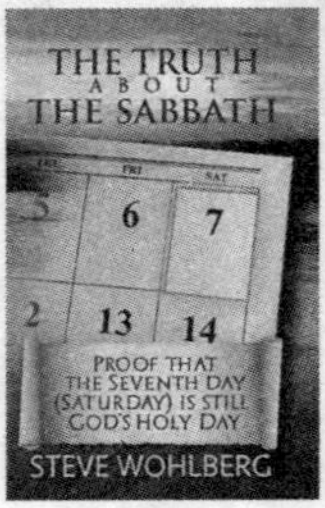

SATAN'S FIRST LIE: EXPOSING GLOBAL MYTHS ABOUT DEATH, GHOSTS, AND THE AFTERLIFE

Most think that when a person dies, only their body returns to dust, while the soul lives on in heaven, or hell, or purgatory, or in the spirit world. Believe it or not, this idea actually originated with a snake in a tree who told Eve that if she sinned, "you will not surely die." Genesis 3:4. Discover the truth about death, burial, resurrection, and a fantastic future beyond the grave.

ORDER FROM

White Horse Media • PO Box 130 • Priest River, ID 83856
1-800-782-4253 • www.WhiteHorseMedia.com

FREE ONLINE BIBLE SCHOOL

Enroll today in White Horse Media's free online Bible school filmed in Israel.
To learn more, visit www.WhiteHorseMediaBibleSchool.com.